大连海事大学校企共建特色教材
大连海事大学–海丰国际教材建设基金资助

U0650795

航运文化

SHIPPING CULTURE

张晓峰 主 编

曾 罡 主 审

大连海事大学出版社
DALIAN MARITIME UNIVERSITY PRESS

图书在版编目（CIP）数据

航运文化：英文／张晓峰主编. —大连 ：大连海
事大学出版社，2024.4
ISBN 978-7-5632-4548-2

Ⅰ．①航…　Ⅱ．①张…　Ⅲ．①航运—文化史—英语
Ⅳ．①F551

中国国家版本馆 CIP 数据核字（2024）第 076915 号

大连海事大学出版社出版

地址：大连市黄浦路523号　邮编：116026　电话：0411-84729665（营销部）　84729480（总编室）
http：//press.dlmu.edu.cn　E-mail：dmupress@ dlmu.edu.cn

大连天骄彩色印刷有限公司印装　　　　　大连海事大学出版社发行

2024 年 4 月第 1 版　　　　　　　　　　2024 年 4 月第 1 次印刷
幅面尺寸：184 mm×260 mm　　　　　　　　　　　　　　印张：10.5
字数：198 千　　　　　　　　　　　　　　　　　印数：1~500 册

出版人：刘明凯

责任编辑：张　冰　　　　　　　　　　　责任校对：席香吉
封面设计：张爱妮　　　　　　　　　　　版式设计：张爱妮

ISBN 978-7-5632-4548-2　　　定价：26.00 元

大连海事大学校企共建特色教材

编 委 会

总前言

航运业是经济社会发展的重要基础产业,在维护国家海洋权益和经济安全、推动对外贸易发展、促进产业转型升级等方面具有重要作用,对我国建设交通强国、海洋强国具有重要意义。大连海事大学作为交通运输部所属的全国重点大学、国家"双一流"建设高校,多年来为我国乃至国际航运业培养了大批高素质航运人才,对航运业的发展起到了重要作用。

进入新时代以来,党中央、国务院及教育主管部门对高等教育的人才培养体系提出了更高要求,对教材工作尤为重视。根据要求,学校大力开展了新工科、新文科等建设及产教融合、科教融合等改革。在教材建设方面,学校修订了教材管理相关制度,建立了校企共建本科教材机制,大力推进校企共建教材工作。其中,航运特色专业的核心课程教材是校企共建的重点,涉及交通运输、海洋工程、物流管理、经济金融、法律等领域。

2021年以来,大连海事大学与海丰国际控股有限公司签订了校企共建教材协议,共同成立了"大连海事大学校企共建特色教材编委会"(简称"编委会"),负责指导、协调校企共建教材相关工作,着力建成一批政治方向正确、满足教学需要、质量水平优秀、航运特色突出、符合国家经济社会发展需求和行业需求的高水平专业核心课程教材。编委会成员主要由大连海事大学校领导和相关领域专家、海丰国际控股有限公司领导和相关行业专家组成。

校企共建特色教材的编写人员经学校二级单位推荐、学校严格审查后确定,均具有丰富的教育教学和教材编写经验,确保了教材的科学性、适用性。公司推荐具有丰富实践经验的行业专家参与共建教材的策划、编写,确保了教材的实践性、前沿性。学校的院、校两级教材工作委员会、党委常委会通过个人审读与会议评审相结合、校内专家与校外专家相结合等不同形式对教材内容进行学术审查和政治审查,确保了教材的学术水平和政治方向。

在校企共建特色教材的编写与出版过程中,海丰国际控股有限公司还向学校提供了经费资助,在此表示感谢。大连海事大学出版社对教材校审、排版等提供了专业的指导与服务,在此表示感谢。同时,感谢各方领导、专家和同仁的大力支持和热情帮助。

校企共建特色教材的编写是一项繁重而复杂的工作,鉴于时间、人力等方面的因素,教材内容难免有不妥之处,希望专家不吝指正。同时,希望更多的航运企事业单位、专家学者能参与到此项工作中来,为我国培养高素质航运人才建言献策。

大连海事大学校企共建特色教材编委会

2022年12月6日

编者的话

大连海事大学英语专业自 2010 年开始开设"航海概论与海事管理"课程至今广受学生的欢迎，我们主要吸纳了目前海事院校讲授"航海概论"和"轮机概论"课程的特点，我们的课程如"蜻蜓点水"般涉及广泛的内容，以满足英语专业学生后续学习海事英语和从事涉海领域的工作需要。

课程建立之初，由于课程设计缺乏内在动力，所以始终没有形成自己的课程特点，因此在 2021 年下半年开始我们拟定了课程的教学大纲，课程性质向着"涉海专业+文化"的新思路，课程也更名为"航运文化"，这一转变符合新文科的融合式思维方式，期望能够走出一条新路。我们在原有讲义的基础上揉进更多的文化因素，在教学设计中注重学生思考，我们又将针对内容思考划分为简单思考和复杂思考两种思考模式，又增加了汉译英与英译汉，以习题练习启发学生积极思考，又紧扣课上讲授的内容。

本教材由张晓峰教授主编，刘新卓高级船长、魏起然船长、李民高级船长作为副主编参与了教材的策划和编写，并在关键业务方面给予指导。王甜甜博士、吕雯钰博士、许琳副教授作为副主编参与了写作的全过程，协助主编对整个教材内容进行梳理，并参与校对工作，王寅春老师、潘琪副教授也参与了教材的编写全过程。整体内容以习近平新时代中国特色社会主义思想为指导，体现了新时代航运的特色，教材内容、关联内容均围绕这一思想核心，大连海事大学外国语学院院长曾罡教授对教材内容进行了审定。本教材在出版过程中得到了大连海事大学教务处和大连海事大学出版社的大力支持，在此一并表示感谢。

编者

2023 年 12 月于大连海事大学心海湖畔

Table of Content
目　录

Chapter One
Historical Navigation Culture

第一章
航海史文化

本章学习目的及本章内容提要

　　航海史文化是航运文化的核心，通过航海史的学习，让学生了解到中国伟大的航海家、外国伟大的航海家。通过航海史了解移民、文化、语言及传统习惯之关联，了解"一带一路"伟大构想的提出背景、"一带一路"参与国家以及"一带一路"和中国古代航海的传承关系。理解以习近平新时代中国特色社会主义思想为指导，新时代航运与世界航运的联系。学习世界航海千年沉淀下来的安全文化的内涵，以及安全与船舶运输行业的关系。

Lesson 1　History of Navigation
第 1 课　航海史

I. Origination of Navigation

Polynesian navigation was probably one of the earliest forms of open-ocean navigation in the foreign navigation world, and it was based on memory and observation recorded on scientific instruments like the Marshall Islands Stick Charts of Ocean Swells. Early Pacific Polynesians used the motion of stars, weather, the position of certain wildlife species, or the size of waves to find the path from one island to another.

Polynesian is the people who live in a division of Oceania including scattered islands of the central and southern Pacific Ocean, roughly between New Zealand, Hawaii, and Easter Island. The larger islands are volcanic, the smaller ones generally coral formations.

In ancient China, the navigation activities started from Emperor Huangdi(黄帝) during 3000 BCE. In *Book of Songs* (诗经), the making of the canoe had been recorded. Two Ministers empowered by Emperor Huangdi to hollow out logs to make canoes and to chip woods to make oars. It is envisaged that the navigation event occurred after the creating of canoe.

II. Ancient Foreign Navigators

Most ancient foreign navigators were born in the age of Great Discoveries of Geography.

1. Christopher Columbus

In the history of navigation of the foreign world, Christopher Columbus is absolutely the first person. He was an explorer, navigator, and colonizer. He was the first European to find a new continent and he also named the American native residents Indians. He was born in Genoa, Italy in 1451 and died on May 20, 1506.

Between 1492 and 1503, Columbus completed four round-trip voyages between Spain and the Americas, each voyage being sponsored by the Crown of Castile. These voyages marked the beginning of the European exploration and colonization of the American continents, and are thus of enormous significance in Western history.

Columbus always insisted, in the face of mounting evidence to the contrary, that the lands that he visited during those voyages were part of the Asian continent, as previously described by Marco Polo and other European traveler. Columbus's refusal to accept that the lands he had visited and claimed for Spain were not part of Asia might explain, in part, why the American continent was named after the Florentine explorer Amerigo Vespucci and not after Columbus.

2. Vasco da Gama

In the period of Columbus's navigation, Portugal was almost strong in navigation. Vasco da Gama persuaded Portuguese King to sponsor his navigation to the Asia. Vasco da Gama was born in Sines, Portugal in 1469 and died in Cochin, India in 1524. He was the first European to journey by sea to India. His epochal voyage (1497 – 1499) was made at the order of Manuel I. With four vessels, he rounded the Cape of Good Hope, passed the easternmost point reached by Bartolomeu Dias in 1488, continued up the east coast of Africa to Malindi, and sailed across the uncharted Indian Ocean to Calicut. This voyage opened up a way for Europe to reach the wealth of the Indies, and immediately Portugal gained great riches from the spice trade; out of it ultimately grew the Portuguese Empire. Gama dictated the instructions for Cabral's voyage (1500 – 1502) to India, and in 1502 he himself led a fleet of 20 ships on his second India voyage. With this force he attempted to establish Portuguese power in Indian waters and sought to secure the submission of a number of chiefs on the African coast. He was harsh in his methods and was not as good an administrator as many of the Portuguese captains who later went to the East, but he was the first, and he was honored with many tributes and the title of count of Vidigueria. In 1524 he was sent back to India as viceroy, but he died soon after his arrival.

3. Ferdinand Magellan

Ferdinand Magellan was born in the Portuguese town of Sabrosa in or around 1480, and he died in Battle of Mactan in Mactan Island of the Philippines on April 27, 1521. He was the commander of the navigation team to complete the voyage of circum navigation. He was the person to name the largest ocean the Peaceful Sea (Now it is called the Pacific Ocean). Magellan became a skilled sailor and naval officer and was in service of the Portuguese crown in Asia. He tried to seek for new route to reach India for navigation, but King Manuel I of Portugal refused to agree on his plan to reach India by a new route, by sailing around the southern end of the South American continent. He sought for another support and was finally supported by King Charles I of Spain to search for a westward route to the Maluku Islands (the "Spice Islands"). Commanding a fleet of five vessels, he headed south through the Atlantic Ocean to Patagonia. Despite a series of storms and mutinies, they made it through the Strait of Magellan into a body of water he named the "peaceful sea" (the modern Pacific Ocean). The expedition reached the Philippine islands, where Magellan was killed during the Battle of Mactan. The expedition later reached the Spice Islands in 1521 and one of the surviving ships eventually returned home via the Indian Ocean, completing the first circuit of the globe.

Magellan had already reached the Malay Archipelago in Southeast Asia on previous voyages travelling east (from 1505 to 1511 – 1512). By visiting this area again but now travelling west, Magellan achieved a nearly complete personal circumnavigation of the globe for the first time in history.

4. James Cook

James Cook was born in the village of Marton in Yorkshire of the UK on November 7, 1728 and he was attacked and killed in 1779 during his third exploratory voyage in the Pacific while attempting to kidnap the ruling chief of the island of Hawaii, Kalaniʻōpuʻu. He commanded three voyages, the first voyage (1768 – 1771), the second voyage (1772 – 1775), and the third voyage (1776 – 1779). As an European, James Cook arrived in Australia in 1770. He was deemed as the first European to find Australia. Before that, Maories are native residents in Australia. James Cook is the person to name the "bagged rat" Kangaroo.

5. Jacques Cartier

Jacques Cartier was born in 1491 in Saint-Malo, the port on the north-east coast of Brittany, France and he died at age 65 on September 1, 1557, during an epidemic, possibly of typhus. Cartier is interred in Saint-Malo Cathedral. He is the first European to find and name Canada, before his discovery, the native residents were American Indians.

III. Ancient Chinese Navigators

In contrast, ancient Chinese navigators started the navigation events for the purpose of the peace and friendship.

1. Xu Fu

Xu Fu, written name Junfang (字君房), was a resident in Langya County (琅琊郡) which a place in the vicinity of Lianyungang City. He was a famous Fangshi(方士) in the Qin Dynasty. According to Biography of the First Emperor Qin in Historical Records (《史记》), written by Sima Qian, 28th year of the First Emperor Qin's (219 BCE), Xufu led a navigation team with 3,000 boys and girls and transited to Japan (瀛洲) to look for longevity medicine for the Emperor. In the history of Japan, it also recorded Xufu's navigation. To some extent, Xufu was the first person to transit the sea and he was the first person to build the friendship between China and Japan.

2.Jianzhen

Buddhist Monk Jianzhen was born in Jiangyang(江阳) of Guangling (广陵) which is called Yangzhou now. In 688 and he died in Japan in 763. Jianzhen is the monk name and his surname is Chunyu (淳于). He tried to transit to Japan six times and he succeeded in transiting at the sixth time. He is deemed as a civil ambassador between Japan and China. He brought medicine, Buddhism to Japan.

3. Zheng He

Zheng He was born in Kunyang of Yunnan Province in 1371 and he died on board his flag ship in 1433. His name was given by Ming Emperor. His original family name was Ma. Zheng He is known as the greatest navigator in ancient China, since his seven voyages were not surpassed at that time. His fleets visited South Asia, Southeast Asia, and East Africa.

Ⅳ. Related Culture Words and Technical Terms

Age of Great Discoveries of Geography（地理大发现时期）—The so-called Age of Great Discoveries of Geography was a period from the early 15th century and continuing into the early 17th century, during which European ships travelled around the world to search for new trading routes and partners to feed burgeoning capitalism in Europe. In the process, Europeans encountered peoples and mapped lands previously unknown to them.

circumnavigate（*v.*）（环球航行）—Sail, fly, or travel completely around the Earth, an island, etc.

colony（*n.*）（殖民地）—A country or an area settled or conquered by people from another country.

latitude（*n.*）（纬度）—The distance of a place north or south of the equator, measured in degrees.

longitude（*n.*）（经度）—The distance east or west of the Greenwich meridian, measured in degrees.

navigation（*n.*）（航海,航行）—The theory and practice of navigating, especially the charting of a course for a ship or an aircraft (It includes traditional navigation, celestial navigation, geo-navigation, and modern navigation.)

navigate（*v.*）（航海,航行）—1580s, a back-formation from navigation, or else from Latin *navigatus*, past participle of *navigare*. Extended to balloons (1784) and later to aircraft (1901). Related: Navigated; navigating. In Latin, navis means ships. Nowadays, navigate means to direct the way that a ship, aircraft, etc. will travel, or to find a direction across, along or over an area of water or land, often by using a map (chart).

adventure（*n.*）（探险）—In navigation, adventure is also the encourage for navigators. It normally refers to a bold and dangerous undertaking of uncertain outcome.

Celestial navigation, astronavigation, cello-navigation（天文航海）— A means of navigation by which a geographical location is determined by reference to the position of celestial bodies. For example, a sextant, a nautical almanac, and a chronometer are capable of position fixing. It was commonly used in the Age of Great Discoveries of Geography.

set sail（开航）—To set the sail into the seat of the sail and get ready for sea. It is common term used in the Age of Sail. Now it is still used to imply that the ship is ready for sea.

log book（船舶日志）—A document used for lodging daily event on board ships. There are deck logbook, radio logbook, engine logbook, and electric logbook. The log was the first tool to record on sailing vessels in ancient time. There was no paper for use. Sailors may scar or paint on the seat of the sail post to record the event.

chart（*n.*）（海图）—Representation of part of ocean or sea for use in navigation. It gives the depth of water, the nature of sea bottom, configuration and characteristics of coast, with positions and brief particulars of navigational aids.

compass(*n.*)（罗经）—Instrument for ascertaining direction, relative to the meridian, by means of magnetic needles, directional gyroscope, or alignment on a known bearing. The last is known as "dumb" compass.

V. Exercises

1. Discuss with your classmates and answer the following questions.

1）How to interpret the "共鼓" "货狄" "刳木为舟,剡木为楫" in English?

2）Why are American Indians called "Indians" now?

3）Describe the voyages of Christopher Columbus.

4）Describe the voyages of Ferdinand Magellan.

5）Describe the voyages of Vasco da Gama.

6）Describe the voyages of James Cook.

7）Describe the voyages of Jacques Cartier.

8）Please find out stories of Xufu in detail.

9）Please find out stories of Jianzhen in more detail.

10）Please find out stories of Zheng He in more detail.

2. Deep thinking

1）What is the major difference between western navigators and Chinese navigators?

2）Why do more nations welcome BRI on the basis of the history of navigation?

3）Why do people in Quebec speak French?

4）Please find the origin of the city name of Vancouver in Canada and tells the relationship with navigation.

5）How come is Kangaroo related to navigation?

6）Explain the death of Ferdinand Magellan and the death of James Cook. What are causes?

7）On the basis of unity（合）and peace（和）, Chinese establish the relationships with other peoples. Please describe more Chinese characteristics.

8）Why did more Europeans wish to arrive in China in the Age of Great Discoveries of Geography?

9）It was said that Christopher Columbus was influenced by Marco Polo. What had been described about China in the Marco Polo's words?

10）Why is it important to complete the circumnavigation?

3. Translate the following sentences into English.

1）郑和下西洋是明代永乐、宣德年间的旷日持久的海上远航活动。之所以称为下西洋,是因为船队首先向南航行,在通过马六甲海峡后向西,而明代中国人习惯把马六甲以西称为西洋,以东称为东洋。郑和首次航行始于永乐三年(1405 年),末次航行结束于宣德八年(1433 年),共计七次。

2）意大利航海家克里斯托弗·哥伦布,生于热那亚,公元 1476 年移居葡萄牙,曾向葡王建议向西航行以探索通往东方印度和中国的海上航路,但未被采纳,1485年他移民西班牙。1492年8月3日,哥伦布奉西班牙统治者伊萨伯拉与斐迪南之命,携带东方君主的图书,率船3只,水手90名,从巴罗斯港出航,横渡大西洋,到达巴哈马群岛、古巴、海地等地。

3)"魁北克"源自阿尔冈昆语词汇"kébec",意指河川收窄之处,后用来指加拿大历史上存在于1763年到1791年的一块北美英国殖民地的名称,传统上是指现魁北克市及其周围地区,亦即圣劳伦斯河收窄至两岸皆面临悬崖的地域。

4)库克船长,是英国皇家海军军官、航海家、探险家和制图师。库克年少时曾于英国商船队服役,1755年加入皇家海军,他参与过七年战争,后来又在魁北克战役期间协助绘制圣劳伦斯河河口大部分地区的地图,战后在1760年左右为纽芬兰岛制作多张精细的地图。

5)罗阿尔德·阿蒙森(1872年7月16日—1928年6月18日),挪威极地探险家。他在探险史上获得了两个"第一",即第一个航行于西北航道,也是第一个到达南极点的航海家。

4. Translate the following sentences into Chinese.

1) At a time when European kingdoms were beginning to establish new trade routes and colonies, motivated by imperialism and economic competition, Columbus proposed to reach the East Indies (South and Southeast Asia) by sailing westward. This eventually received the support of the Spanish Crown, which saw a chance to enter the spice trade with Asia through this new route. During his first voyage in 1492, he reached the New World instead of arriving at Japan as he had intended, landing on an island in the Bahamas archipelago that he named "San Salvador". Over the course of three more voyages, he visited the Greater and Lesser Antilles, as well as the Caribbean coast of Venezuela and Central America, claiming all of it for the Crown of Castile.

2) In the voyages, Cook sailed thousands of miles across largely uncharted areas of the globe. He mapped lands from New Zealand to Hawaii in the Pacific Ocean in greater detail and on a scale not previously charted by Western explorers. He surveyed and named features, and recorded islands and coastlines on European maps for the first time. He displayed a combination of seamanship, superior surveying and cartographic skills, physical our age, and an ability to lead men in adverse conditions.

3) On April 20, 1534, Cartier set sail under a commission from the king, hoping to discover a western passage to the wealthy markets of Asia. In the words of the commission, he was to "discover certain islands and lands where it is said that a great quantity of gold and other precious things are to be found". It took him twenty days to sail across the ocean. Starting on May 10 of that year, he explored parts of Newfoundland, the Strait of Belle Isle and southern shore of the Labrador Peninsula, the Gaspé and North Shore coast lines on the Gulf of St. Lawrence, and some parts of the coasts of the Gulf's main islands, including Prince Edward Island, Anticosti Island and the Magdalen Islands. During one stop at lesaux Oiseaux (Islands of the Birds, now the Rochers-aux-Oiseaux federal bird sanctuary,

northeast of Brion Island in the Magdalen Islands), his crew slaughtered around 1,000 birds, most of them great auks (extinct since 1852). Cartier's first two encounters with aboriginal peoples in Canada on the north side of Chaleur Bay, most likely the Mi'kmaq, were brief; some trading occurred.

4) Wang Dayuan, courtesy name Huanzhang was a traveler from Quanzhou, China during the Yuan Dynasty in the 14th century. He is known for his two major ship voyages. During 1328 – 1333, he sailed along the South China Sea, and visited many places in Southeast Asia. He reached as far as South Asia and Australia, and landed in modern-day Bengal, Sri Lanka, and India, as well as areas close to modern-day Darwin, Australia. In 1334–1339, he visited North Africa and East Africa. Around 1330, Wang visited the island of Singapore, where he wrote about a small settlement called *Danmaxi* (Malay: *Temasek*) that had both Malay and Chinese residents, and already had an established China town. His 1349 account of his travel, *DaoYi ZhiLue* (《岛夷志略》), is one of the few records documenting the early history of Singapore.

5) Vasco da Gama was a Portuguese explorer and the first European to reach India by sea. His initial voyage to India (1497 – 1499) was the first to link Europe and Asia by an ocean route, connecting the Atlantic and the Indian oceans and therefore, the West and the Orient. This is widely considered a milestone in world history, as it marked the beginning of a sea-based phase of global multiculturalism. Da Gama's discovery of the sea route to India opened the way for an age of global imperialism and enabled the Portuguese to establish along-lasting colonial empire in Asia. The violence and hostage taking employed by da Gama and those who followed also assigned a brutal reputation to the Portuguese among India's indigenous kingdoms that would set the pattern for western colonialism in the Age of Exploration. Travelling the ocean route allowed the Portuguese to avoid sailing across the highly disputed Mediterranean and traversing the dangerous Arabian Peninsula. The sum of the distances covered in the outward and return voyages made this expedition the longest ocean voyage ever made until then, far longer than a full voyage around the world by way of the Equator.

Lesson 2　Unique Shipping Under the BRI
第 2 课　"一带一路"下中国特色航运

I. Background and Importance of Old Silk Road

The Old Silk Road or Silk Route is a historical network of interlinking trade routes across the Afro-Eurasian landmass that connected East, South, and Western Asia with the Mediterranean and European world, as well as parts of North and East Africa. The Silk Road includes routes through Syria, Turkey, Iran, Turkmenistan, Uzbekistan, Kyrgyzstan, Pakistan and China. In ancient China, peaceful thoughts were in mind. Peace (和) and Unity (合) are two important cultural elements in ancient Chinese' mind.

Extending 4,000 miles (6,437 kilometres), the Silk Road gets its name from the lucrative Chinese silk trade which was carried out along its length, and began during the Han Dynasty (202 BCE – 220 CE). The central Asian sections of the trade routes were expanded around 114 BCE by the Han Dynasty, largely through the missions and explorations of Zhang Qian (张骞), but earlier trade routes across the continents already existed.

Trade on the Silk Road was a significant factor in the development of the civilizations of China, the Indian subcontinent, Persia, Europe and Arabia. Though silk was certainly the major trade item from China, many other goods were traded, and various technologies, religions and philosophies, as well as the bubonic plague (the "Black Death"), also traveled along the Silk Routes.

Routes of Zheng He's seven voyages are the old maritime silk roads. Empowered by Ming Emperor Yong Le, Zheng He (郑和), a mariner, diplomat, fleet admiral, led the large fleets to visit southeast countries, south Asia countries, and east Africa countries. Such places like Brunei, Java, Thailand, Southeast Asia, India, the Horn of Africa, and Arabia. They built businesses, dispensing and receiving goods along the way. Zheng He presented gifts of gold, silver, porcelain, and silk, and in return, China received such novelties as ostriches, zebras, camels, and ivory from the Swahili Coast. The giraffe that he brought back from Malindi was considered to be a qilin and taken as proof of the Mandate of Heaven upon the administration. The Daxuexi Alley Mosque in Xi'an has a stele dating to January 1523, inscribed with Zheng He's the fourth maritime voyage to Tianfang, Arabian Peninsula.

II. BRI and the Significance of the BRI

While we are in the period of building period under Socialism with Chinese characteristics, the BRI, short as the Belt and Road Initiative plays an important role in the shipping industry. The Belt and Road Initiative put forward by President Xi Jinping in 2013 is of great importance to the world shipping. It is a great initiative to make mutual benefits among nations or regions. It is a cooperative mode to let other peoples to share the economic achievements under the Open Policy of China. The strong and prosperous China plays an important role in the world shipping. The BRI economic zone is one of the world economic powers to drive the world shipping increasing. The following countries or regions participate in the BRI building, including Niger, Comoros, Benin, Lesotho, Solomon Islands, Mali, Equatorial Guinea, Liberia, Peru, Cyprus, Jamaica, Luxembourg, Italy, Cuba, Barbados, Vanuatu, Ecuador, Portugal, Tonga, Cook Islands, Micronesia, Fiji, Malta, El Salvador, Dominican Republic, Chile, Samoa, Suriname, Grenada, Venezuela, Togo, Gambia, Uganda, Cape Verde, Burundi, Tanzania, Zimbabwe, Congo, Chad, Nigeria, Kenya, Angola, Namibia, Gabon, Mozambique, Zambia, Ghana, Seychelles, South Sudan, Cameroon, Sierra Leone, Cote d'Ivoire, Algeria, Costa Rica, Djibouti, Mauritania, Guinea, Somalia, Greece, Uruguay, Niue, Dominica, Guyana, Rwanda, Senegal, Tunisia, Libya, Papua, New Guinea, Bolivia, Antigua and Barbuda, Trinidad and Tobago, Austria, Madagascar, Panama, Morocco, Ethiopia, Sudan, New Zealand, Bosnia and Herzegovina, Montenegro, Turkmenistan, Palestine, Albania, Afghanistan, Pakistan, Slovenia, Croatia, Lebanon, Oman, Bahrain, Yemen, Egypt, Jordan, Syria, Indonesia, Philippines, Myanmar, Brunei, Timor-Leste, Bhutan, United Arab Emirates, Thailand, Viet Nam, Singapore, Israel, Azerbaijan, Armenia, Bangladesh, Belarus, Cambodia, Georgia, Hungary, Iraq, Iran, Kyrgyzstan, Laos, Kazakhstan, Qatar, Kuwait, Moldova, Maldives, Malaysia, Macedonia, Mongolia, Nepal, Poland, Bulgaria, Romania, Serbia, Saudi Arabia, Slovakia, Tajikistan, Russia, South Africa, Sri Lanka, Republic of Korea, Turkey, Ukraine, and Uzbekistan.

"The Belt and Road Initiative provides an important platform for building a global community of shared future. To make a real success of the BRI, it is imperative to follow the Silk Road spirit characterized by peace and cooperation, openness and inclusiveness, mutual learning, and mutual benefit. It is also important to focus on policy coordination, connectivity of infrastructure, unimpeded trade, financial integration, and closer people-to-people ties. It is essential to uphold the principles of extensive consultation, joint contribution, and shared benefits, and to pursue open, green, clean, and close cooperation to improve people's lives and promote sustainable development. The BRI has turned ideas into actions and vision into reality, and the initiative itself is a public product widely welcomed by the international community. China has signed more than 200 documents on BRI cooperation with 140 countries and 32 international organizations. A World Bank report shows that the BRI could contribute to lifting 7.6 million people from extreme poverty and 32 million from moderate poverty, boost trade by 2.8 to 9.7 percent for participating countries and by 1.7 to 6.2 percent for the world, and increase global incomes by 0.7 to 2.9 percent. The BRI originated in China, but the opportunities and benefits it creates belong to the world. It pursues development, advocates win-win cooperation, and conveys hope."

Ⅲ. Asian Infrastructure Investment Bank (AIIB)

Under the initiative of President Xi Jinping on October 2, 2013, Asian Infrastructure Investment Bank established. On October 24, 2014, 21 Finance Minister from creative countries signed in Beijing to build the AIIB. On March 12, 2015, the UK applied to participate in the AIIB. Thereafter, France, Germany, Italy applied to participate in. It provides the investments for infrastructure building. The first assembly of the Council and Board of Directors of AIIB was held in Beijing during 16th and 18th of January, 2016.

Ⅳ. Project Under the BRI

China had already assisted other countries to build port facilities. For example, China had built Gwadar Port for Pakistan and it had been in service since March 20, 2007. That is one of the typical samples for China to help developing countries to build infrastructures. It brings benefits for other nations. The other example shows China participated in building of Port of Piraeus, the largest port in Greece. Since the economy in Greece is not in good situation, China puts funds in the port building. Under the building of the Port, Greece's economic growth booms accordingly. It is one of the largest relay ports in the world.

The BRI plays a significant role in the world shipping, since it is to show that a community with shared future for mankind. In other word, the world belongs to all human beings. The BRI building meets the requirements of all peoples and nations. Therefore a lot of countries participated in the BRI building.

Since China proposed the BRI in 2013, more than 3,000 cooperation projects have been launched, involving investment of nearly $1 trillion and creating 420,000 jobs for participating countries, the Foreign Ministry said. As a result, many nations have realized their dreams of building railways and large bridges, and also of alleviating poverty.

The Belt and Road Initiative has "endless potential" to benefit all, said an expert at a Serbian research institute.

Ⅴ. Related Culture Words and Technical Terms

shipping (*n.*) (航运,船舶)—1. The act or business of transporting goods; 2. The body of ships belonging to one port, industry, or country, often referred to in aggregate tonnage; 3. Passage or transport on a ship.

Maritime Silk Road (海上丝绸之路)—It is a sea route between China and other countries in ancient times. It also refers to Maritime Porcelain Route and Maritime Spice

Route. It originated from the Shang and Zhou Dynasty and it was developing in the period of Spring and Autumn as well as Warring States. It was fixed in the Qin and Han Dynasty. The high peak is in the Ming Dynasty. The voyages of Zheng He's fleet are the Maritime Silk Road. There are two main roads. One is southward and the other is eastward.

Economic Zone (经济带)—It is a region under special common interests. It is a concept on the basis of economy and geography. For example, the China-Pakistan Economic Corridor (CPEC), is the economically geographical area, since there are cooperative projects operating in this zone.

Belt and Road (一带一路)—Belt and Road (B & R) is the short term for building of economic zone of 21st century silk road and 21st century maritime silk road. President Xi Jinping put forward the initiative in September and October, 2013. It offers great opportunities to world shipping industry.

Five Links (五通)—The five links are five *tong*s (通) in Chinese. Five aspects include policy, facility, trade, finance, and peoples. It refers to on policy coordination (政策沟通), connectivity of infrastructure (设施联通), unimpeded trade (贸易畅通), financial integration (资金融通), and closer people-to-people ties (民心相通).

VI. Exercises

1. Discuss with your classmates and answer the following questions.

1) Why is the BRI welcomed by different peoples?

2) How will you make contributions in the BRI building, as an English major student?

3) What does "initiative" mean in the BRI?

4) Give examples of the BRI projects.

5) Describe the story of Zhangqian.

6) When did President Xi Jinping recommend the BRI?

7) What does AIIB stand for?

8) What does the abbreviation CPEC stand for?

9) Please pick up the country names with suffix "-stan" and explain the relationships.

10) In geography, a state in the United States and a country share the same name. What are they?

2. Deep thinking.

1) Read the countries participating in the BRI and explain the BRI economic zone.

2) Why do we think the peaceful environment is the condition of economic building?

3) Discuss the relationship between the BRI and the global community of shared future.

4) Explain "Five Links" in your comprehension.

5) China's economy has been developing dramatically since 1980s. What is the force for such successful achievement?

6) Please comment your understanding on "和" and "合".

7) Please draw a map and explain the routes of B&I. Explain the influence to the

international shipping.

8）Describe the Maritime Silk Road.

9）Explain the important roles of Chinese Transport in international shipping.

10）What are the peculiar properties of Shipping in China?

3. Translate the following sentences into English.

1）"一带一路"是"丝绸之路经济带"和"21世纪海上丝绸之路"的简称,2013年9月和10月由中国国家主席习近平分别提出建设"丝绸之路经济带"和"21世纪海上丝绸之路"的合作倡议。依靠中国与有关国家既有的双多边机制,借助既有的、行之有效的区域合作平台,一带一路旨在借用古代丝绸之路的历史符号,高举和平发展的旗帜,积极发展与沿线国家的经济合作伙伴关系,共同打造政治互信、经济融合、文化包容的利益共同体、命运共同体和责任共同体。

2）丝绸之路是起始于古代中国,连接亚洲、非洲和欧洲的古代陆上商业贸易路线,最初的作用是运输古代中国出产的丝绸、瓷器等商品,后来成为东方与西方之间在经济、政治、文化等诸多方面进行交流的主要道路。

3）海上丝绸之路,是指古代中国与世界其他地区进行经济文化交流交往的海上通道,最早开辟也始于秦汉时期。从广州、泉州、宁波、扬州等沿海城市出发,从南洋到阿拉伯海,甚至远达非洲东海岸的海上贸易的"海上丝绸之路"。

4）在中国共产党的正确领导下,中国航运自中华人民共和国成立开始,逐步完善,并实现了跨世纪的历史大发展,国际航运、国内航运、集装箱运输、航运服务业、港口服务、水运基础设施建设与维护、海事监管与搜救等内容均走在前列。

5）中国的航运自20世纪初期开始即走上了世界航运舞台的中央,中国航运方案,中国的航运法规对全世界的航运治理等方面起到了主导作用。

4. Translate the following sentences into Chinese.

1）COSCO SHIPPING Development Co., Ltd., stylized as COSCO SHIPPING Development is a financial services company based in Shanghai, China. It was known as CHINA SHIPPING Container Lines（CSCL）and was among the world's largest container liner companies. It exited the container shipping business and was renamed to COSCO SHIPPING Development because of the COSCO-China Shipping merger in 2016.

2）After China joined the WTO in 2001, CSCL grew rapidly, playing a major role in supporting China's economic advancement and international trade. With continued support from the Chinese government, CSCL's global TEU market share increased 126% between 2000 and 2006, becoming the second fastest growing container carrier in the world. In 2004, CSCL became the world's tenth largest ocean container line in terms of TEU capacity, and in 2007, it became the world's sixth largest. In 2005, CSCL was named the "World's Most Profitable Container Liner Company" by the journal American Shipper. In 2007 and again in 2008, Long Beach Port Authority awarded CSCL the "Honor of Environmental Protection". In 2009, CSCL was awarded the "Best Annual Carrier" by Michaels Stores.

3）Recently, a container ship loaded with shrimp slices, melons and aquatic products departed from the seaport of Muara in Brunei to Qinzhou Port in South China's Guangxi

Zhuang autonomous region, with the cargo to be delivered by rail later to Southwest China for sale. Muara Port is Brunei's largest port, while Qinzhou Port in the Beibu Gulf is an important hub for trade and economic exchanges between China and the member states of the Association of Southeast Asian Nations.

4) The recently built OOCL Piraeus, one of the largest container vessels in the world, received a water salute on July 10 as it arrived at the Port of Piraeus in Greece, a major hub among the economies involved in the 10-year-old Belt and Road Initiative. The port, run by Chinese shipping giant COSCO SHIPPING, hosted a visit by President Xi Jinping in 2019 and is among the over 3,000 cooperative programs within the BRI framework. Chinese Ambassador to Greece Xiao Junzheng said the European nation is a major portal for the rest of the world to access the continent, and "well-developed land-sea transportation architecture plays a key part" in tapping into the geographical advantages of the country.

5) The global landscape is swiftly evolving into a multiplex world defined by multiple modernities, diverse civilizations and multiple power centers. This is an interconnected and interdependent world where both state and non-state actors interact to shape the emerging international order. The relationship between the Association of Southeast Asian Nations and China is evolving within this dynamic. The geographical proximity between the ASEAN member states and China has served as a foundation in shaping their relations and facilitating frequent interactions, exchanges and cooperation at various levels. This proximity has not only encouraged the development of robust diplomatic ties but has also allowed for the easy movement of people, goods and ideas between the ASEAN members and China. The shared land borders, maritime routes and immediate regional presence have created an environment conducive to sustained engagement and collaboration, fostering a sense of familiarity and mutual understanding.

Lesson 3   Safety and Security Culture in Shipping
第 3 课   航运安全文化

I . Safety and Security Concept

Safety means being safe or not being dangerous, or not in danger. In the early 14th century, safety is written as *sauvete*. It means safety, safeguard; salvation; security, surety in Old French. Safety, as the accident-prevention slogan, was first recorded in 1873.

Security means freedom or protection from danger or worry; or measures taken to prevent spying, attacks, theft, etc. Security was in English in the middle 15 century. It was borrowed from Latin word "*securitas*". In the early 13 century, it was *sikerhede* or *sikenesse*. In modern French, the security is written *securité*.

Safety and security are similar and they are translated into Chinese "安全". Safety problem may connect to safety accident, such as fire, explosion, personal injury. Security problem may relate to security problem, such as armed robbery, piracy, or kidnap.

II . Safety and Security Culture

In shipping industry, safety culture is the first culture. Safety-first culture is the foundation. In marine industry, making money will be on the basis of safety and security. SOLAS, the international convention for the safety of life at sea.

In IMO's opinion, "Shipping is perhaps the most international of all the world's great industries—and it is one of the most dangerous. It has always been recognized that the best way of improving safety at sea is by developing international regulations that are followed by all shipping nations. " The IMO working slogan is, "safe, secure, efficient shipping on clean oceans."

Therefore, safety and security become the first factor to be considered in the shipping industry. The IMO had implemented the ISM code to focus on the safe operation of ships and marine pollution prevention from ships in 1994. Safety and Security are the core of safety culture. In the shipping industry, safety goes first. Safety is the centre of all activities. DPA, short for designated person ashore, is the person nominated by the top leader. The DPA is responsible for running safety management system in the shipping industry. In other word, the DPA is the leader of the safety system. ISPS, short for the international ship and port facility security code, is the convention regarding security problems. In accordance with the ISPS,

CSO, short for Company Security Officer, is responsible for security issues for the shipping company. SSO, short for Ship Security Officer, is responsible for security issues for the ship. PFSO, short for Port Facility Security Officer, is responsible for the security issues for the port or berth. Since the ISM code and the ISPS code are related to safety and security, both codes are attached to the SOLAS convention.

III. Safety and Security Drills

One of safety and security measures is the drills. Under the SOLAS convention, every ship is required to organise drills and exercises concerning safety and security. The safety drills include fire drill, boat drill, pollution prevention drill and man-overboard drill. The security drill includes anti-piracy. Drills are a part of safety culture, and the drills are to be executed monthly. Emergency sound signals are to be familarised. For example, seven short blasts followed by one prolonged blast are the general emergency alarm. Three prolonged blasts are the signals for man overboard. One short blast and followed by two prolonged blasts and then followed by one short blast are the sound alarm for pollution. Short blasts lasting one minute and then followed by prolonged blast(s) are the fire drill. The prolonged blast represents the location in the fire drill. One prolonged blast means the fire on the forecastle while two prolonged blasts means the fire in the middle. Three prolonged blasts means the fire at the stern while four prolonged blasts refers to the fire in the engine room. Five prolonged blasts means the fire on deck. Drills are often scenarios to practice the procedure in the emergency. All persons involved shall attend the drills. On board a ship, the composite drills will be executed monthly. The Shipmaster will be the general leader and the Shipmaster will be on the bridge to command, control, coordinate the entire drill and the Chief Officer will be the leader on spot to carry out the orders from the Shipmaster. While the fire in the engine room, the Chief Engineer is the leader on spot and the Chief Engineer will standby in the engine control room and the Second Engineer will work on spot.

IV. Certification, Documentation and Records

Certification means to certify the shipping industry or the ships to verify that the unity attains the standards under international maritime conventions, regulations, laws, rules, or codes.

1. Safety Documentation

In ISM system, the documentation system includes the Safety Management Manuals under the Safety Management System are to be set up under the ISM code. The maritime unity may will establish a safety system, including documents. The SMM will be run by the shipping industry. The Internal Audits will be carried out all the time. On the other hand, the Administration will arrange the external audits to verify the implementation of the ISM code. The Administration will issue the DOC to the company as long as the company meets the requirement and issue the SMC to a particular ship providing that the ship in the company meets the requirement of the ISM code.

Documentation and records are the practice in the safety culture, which means all events are to be logged. In the running of ISM code, the non-conformity report (NCR) shall be reported to the shipping company. The review records in the running of the ISM code are also necessary.

2. Security Culture

In the running of ISPS code, the certification from the Administration is required for issuing to the shipping industry. The International Ship Security Certificate (ISSC) is the certificate issued to the shipping companies upon the compliance with the ISPS code. The Document of Security (DoS) is the written form to declare the compliance with the ISPS code. The Ship Security Plan (SSP) is made for drills as well as the implementation of the ISPS code.

All in all, certifications and records are approaches to achieve safety and security.

V. Related Culture Words and Technical Terms

no record, no action (无记录,则无行为)—It is a common sense to show the importance of record. It says that all shipping industries will follow the record rules. All events will be recorded in the logbooks, records, manuals, checklists.

checklist (*n.*) (检查单)—A procedure to show the completion of a key operation by breaking down the entire steps into separated ones. Each step will be checked and confirmed.

safety first (安全第一)—It means the benefits after safety. While the ship is at sea, the most significant thing to be considered is the safety.

Your ship is the best lifeboat (你船就是最好的救生艇)—It is a concept to recommend that the crewmembers should cherish safety on board. Albeit the lifeboat can be used to evacuate from the mother ship, that is not 100% safe.

occupational safety (职务安全) **and occupational safety equipment** (职务安全设备)—Occupational safety refers to the safety for working. The occupational safety equipment is the equipment for the purpose of safe working. Examples are helmets, goggles, safety harnesses, safety boots, overalls, gloves, etc.

safety meeting (安全会)—It belongs to the safety culture on board. In general, the ship will organize safety meeting monthly. The Shipmaster may organize the ship safety meeting. In addition, the Chief Officer will organize the safety meeting for deck department whereas the Chief Engineer will organize the safety meeting for engine department.

LSA (救生设施)—LSA stands for life saving appliance. It includes lifeboats, liferafts, lifebuoys, lifejackets, and rescue boats.

FFA (消防设备)—FFA stands for fire-fighting appliance. It is also called as fire-fighting equipment. It includes monitors, detectors, water hydrants, fixed installation, international shore connectors, fire alarms, etc.

BTT (班前会)—BTT refers to box, tools, and talk. It belongs to the safety culture on board. It shows that the communications on safety shall be completed prior to work.

PTWS（工作许可证制度）—PTWS refers to permit-to-work scheme. Each critical operation shall be well prepared by all operators. Merely will the operation be performed under the permit from the Shipmaster.

VI. Exercises

1. Discuss with your classmates and answer the following questions.

1）What does the ISM mean?

2）What does the ISPS mean?

3）What is the background of the ISPS code?

4）What are relationships among the CSO, the SSO, and the PFSO?

5）List some records used on board.

6）Why do ships organize daily safety meetings in common practice?

7）Please make a paragraph with sentences starting with the letter S, A, F, E, T, Y.

8）Before a Chinese student went to school, the parents may say "LU SHANG ZHU YI ANQUAN!（路上注意安全）" What does "ANQUAN"（安全）really mean?

9）Why are appliance used in the LSA and the FFA?

10）What is the relationship between the English word security and the French word securité?

2. Deep thinking.

1）What is the deep cause on terrorist attacks of September 11, 2001?

2）What measures will be taken to protect personal security in our daily life?

3）Please explain the relationships between the IMO slogan and the international maritime conventions.

4）When you first come on board a ship, what is the first thing will you consider?

5）What are unsafe cases on the common sense? Please list some.

6）What is your translation version for "安全第一,预防为主"?

7）Who is the DPA at your university or college? What are roles of the DPA?

8）Before crewmembers enter into confined spaces or enclosed spaces, what will they think about?

9）What are roles of scenario for a lifeboat drill or a fire-fighting drill?

10）What will the Ship Security Officer do when a security accident incurred on board?

3. Translate the following sentences into English.

1)《中华人民共和国船舶安全监督规则》的制定原则是为了保障水上人命、财产安全,防止船舶造成水域污染,规范船舶安全监督工作,依据相关法规,其规则适用于对中国籍船舶和水上设施以及航行、停泊、作业于我国管辖水域的外国籍船舶实施的安全监督工作,并遵循依法、公正、诚信、便民的原则。

2)安全是海运的前提,如果没有安全,船舶随时都有可能灭失,船员的生命就无法保障,而船上的财产安全也将得不到保障。对于唯利是图而不考虑安全的船舶所有人,最终会被社会的巨轮所碾压。

3）船舶的安全科学是由"人、机、环境、控制"构成的系统。船员属于"人"要素，而船舶与货物属于"机"因素，换言之就是"物"要素。航道与港口属于"环境要素"，而船公司等属于"管理"也就是"控制"要素。

4）船舶安全许可证制度系指船舶在进行重大操作前需要对船舶安全状况进行评估，并按照安全要素填写检查单。评估表格需要提交给船长，并由船长签字批准。凡是船长不签字的操作将不能实施。

5）安全不仅仅是手段，更是保障。只有在船舶足够安全的前提下，船舶的运输和其他操作才能进行，船舶不论何时何地都不能主动选择进入不安全操作，而且当事故发生后，也要采取积极措施脱险。

4. Translate the following sentences into Chinese.

1）In so far as the Company is an employer on board ship, it has a duty to assess the risks to workers and others affected by its activities. The Company's activity is the operation of the ship, and so it is responsible for coordinating the control measures identified in the risk assessments of all other relevant employers on board, as appropriate.

2）Employers are required to ensure the health and safety of workers and other persons so far as possible, by the application of certain principles, including the evaluation of unavoidable risks and the taking of action to reduce them. Specifically, employers are required to make a suitable and sufficient assessment of the risks to health and safety of workers arising in the normal course of their activities or duties, for the purpose of identifying.

3）All workers should be subject to whatever health surveillance is appropriate for the work activities they are involved in. Examples of circumstances in which it may be useful include: exposure to hazardous substances, working with vibrating tools, exposure to high levels of noise, use of substances known to cause dermatitis (e.g. solvent) and exposure to certain dusts (e.g. asbestos)

4）The safety officer must maintain a record of all accidents and dangerous occurrences. On a ship where no safety officer is appointed, this duty falls to the Company. These records must be made available on request to any safety representative, the Shipmaster or to any person duly authorized by the Secretary of State.

5）Handling and storage of garbage can present health and safety hazards to crews and ships. Requirements of the garbage management plan should be observed. Particular attention should be paid to the correct methods of disposal of waste oils (bilge or other), chemicals, galley waste, garbage (especially plastics, glass, drums and other non-biodegradable items), and redundant items (moorings, dunnage, cargo cleanings, etc.). Incinerators and compactors should always be operated by competent personnel, and operating instructions should be strictly followed.

Chapter Two
Blame Culture

第二章
责罚文化

本章学习目的及本章内容提要

　　通过本章学习了解海上责罚文化的独特现象，辨识陆地赏识文化与海上责罚文化之间的区别与联系。掌握国际海事组织、国际航运组织、船旗国政府对船舶行业的"齐抓共管"现象，了解木桶短板原理与责罚文化的关联。了解责罚理念指导下航运业对船舶进行的各类检查。了解船舶文件和船员个人文件的格式、文件发放形式、文件的保管方式、文件丢失等处理方式。

Lesson 4　Introductions to Appreciative Culture and Blame Culture
第4课　赏识文化和责罚文化

I. Appreciative Culture

The Appreciative Culture is the main culture used in modern society. The word appreciative is an adjective which means feeling or showing that you enjoy something or are pleased about it. If someone is morally responsible for doing something right, we may say that his or her action is praiseworthy. That is the culture used in the education system. We may say the Appreciative Culture is the culture in our mind. When you are doing something right, you may hope others will appreciate your doings. The Appreciative Culture is useful to foster qualified persons on land. In contrast, the Blame Culture is another culture used in the maritime field.

II. Blame Culture

In your childhood, your parents might punish you because of wrongdoing or improper behaviour. Some fathers are fault finders because they try to seek the children's faults. That is called the Blame Culture.

Blame is the act of censuring, holding responsible making negative statements about an individual or group that their action or actions are socially or morally irresponsible, the opposite of praise. When someone is morally responsible for doing something wrong, their action is blameworthy. The maritime culture is just a type of the Blame Culture.

III. Culture Differences

The Appreciative Culture is much positive and it stands on the positive foundation. The assessed unit or part is supposed to be a right-doing one. While it is evaluated, the good part will be picked up. To pick up right-doing parts is to make confidence for the doer. In fact, no one can be the perfect person. The doer will be encouraged, as long as the doer does the right thing.

On the other hand, the Blame Culture is used for picking up the wrongdoing. The assessor assumes that the doer must have weaknesses. In other word, the assessor stands on the negative point. Also, no one can be the perfect person. The doer will be punished, as long as the doer did a wrong thing.

One coin has two sides. Each culture has its own advantages and disadvantages. The Shipowners may combine both cultures. For example, they may pay bounsers to right doer and punish the wrong doer in common practice.

Ⅳ. Importance of Blame Culture

In modern society, there are laws, rules, codes, and regulations. Those are the restrictions or limitations to show people shall obey those. Otherwise, the units or persons who violated will be punished.

The shipping industry is much valuable. While doing something wrong, the losses or damages are huge. In that case, the Blame Culture is a lever to control substandard. In fact, the water height in the drum depends on the shortest wooden board. While the serve weakness (shortest wooden board) is found, the condition (water height) is evaluated. In that case, the surveys, inspections, audits, checks, tests, and examinations will be carried out for the unit. In common sense, the unit refers to the ship, as the ship is a basic part of the shipping industry.

Ⅴ. Related Culture Words and Technical Terms

survey (*n.*) (检验)—The inspection made by the classification society to evaluate the condition of the ship.

Administration (*n.*) (主管机关)—The competent authority for maritime safety administration.

punish (*vt.*) (惩罚)—To hurt, imprison, fine, etc. somebody for wrongdoing.

sanction (*n.*) (处罚)—A penalty, specified or in the form of moral pressure, that acts to ensure compliance or conformity. A coercive measure, adopted usually by several parties acting together against a party violating international law.

substandard (*a.*) (低标准)—Below standard or less than adequate. In general, it is a term used in PSC.

classification society care (船级社管理)—In common practice, almost all ships are cared by the relevant classification societies. The classification societies will give technical advice to ships.

verbs for inspection (检查的动词)—A package of verbs can be used to show the inspections on ships, for example, control, inspect, survey, supervise, surveillance, monitor, administrate.

MoU (备忘录)—MoU refers to memorandum of understanding. It is a document describing a bilateral or multilateral agreement between two or more parties. It expressed a convergence of will between parties, indicating an intended common line of action. It is often used in cases where parties either do not imply a legal commitment or in situations where the parties create a legally enforceable agreement. It is a more formal alternative to a gentlemen's agreement.

VI. Exercises

1. Discuss with your classmates and answer the following questions.

1) What do you think the Appreciative Culture?

2) What do you think the Blame Culture?

3) Explain the Appreciative Culture as the examples.

4) Explain the Blame Culture as the examples.

5) What is the difference between the evaluation systems for the shipping industry and the society on shore?

6) In English, the term "try the limit" is used. Please explain the causes.

7) How important is the inspection of the association?

8) Why do you think the Blame Culture is suitable for maritime field?

9) What is the purpose of the safety inspection for the shipping industry?

10) Can you describe the characteristic differences between your father and your mother?

2. Deep thinking.

1) Please describe the disadvantages of the blame culture.

2) Say your idea on "Spare the rod and spoil the child".

3) Do you think that the parent has the right to punish the son or daughter? Why or why not?

4) Please describe the dissimilarity between the campus culture and ship culture in your opinion.

5) How is the Blame Culture related to the PSC, the FSC, the association inspections, the CS survey, the immigration inspection, and customs inspection?

6) Please explain the "drum theory" and explain the relationships between the theory and the Blame Culture.

7) In the shipping industry, the evaluation may be simply described as standard or substandard. In the school education system, the evaluation may be classified into excellent, good, fair, pass, or not pass. Can you explain the similarities and dissimilarities?

8) Can you memorize the last punishment made by one of your parents?

9) What is favourable for education, appreciative culture or blame culture?

10) In traditional education, the teacher used the ferule (戒尺) to punish the student. Describe the culture.

3. Translate the following sentences into English.

1) 责罚文化是航运界的主流文化,其精髓就是检查者在船舶操作中找到问题的弱项,以弥补缺陷。

2) 依照国际海事公约进行检查,查出缺陷是责罚文化最好的体现之一,同样责罚文化另外一个尺度,就是采用"合格"或者"不合格"。在日常赏识文化中的优秀、良好等更高层次分级并不适用于责罚文化。

3）滞留船舶是惩罚低标准船舶的最严厉的处罚方式之一，该做法就是不准船舶开航。

4）检查人员必须熟悉检查理念、操作程序、人文背景等，检查的本身是检查文化的一种表现形式。

5）船旗国监督系指船舶注册国家主管机关对船舶安全运营的一种监督检查，检查的主要标准是国内相关海事法规以及国际海事公约。

4. Translate the following sentences into Chinese.

1）PSC is a ship inspection program whereby foreign ships entering a sovereign state's waters are boarded and inspected to ensure compliance with various major international maritime conventions. PSC programs are of a regional nature, that is, several countries sharing common waters have grouped together under a MoU to ensure that vessels trading in there are not substandard.

2）In international relations, MoUs fall under the broad category of treaties and should be registered in the United Nations treaty database. In practice and in spite of the United Nations' Legal Section insistence that registration be done to avoid "secret diplomacy", MoUs are sometimes kept confidential.

3）The primary responsibility for ensuring that a ship maintains a standard at least equivalent to that specified in international conventions rests with the Flag State, and if all Flag States performed their duties satisfactorily there would be no need for Port State Control.

4）Courses of action a PSCO may impose on a ship with deficiencies (in order of ascending gravity)：Deficiencies can be rectified within 14 days for minor infractions. Under specific conditions, deficiencies can be rectified when the ship arrives at the next port. Deficiencies must be rectified before the ship can depart from the port. The ship is detained.

5）The objective of the ship classification is to verify the structural strength and integrity of essential parts of the ship's hull and its appendages, and the reliability and function of the propulsion and steering systems, power generation and those other features and auxiliary systems that have been built into the ship in order to maintain essential services on board. Classification Societies aim to achieve the objective through the development and application of their rules and by verifying compliance with international and/or national statutory regulations on behalf of Flag Administrations.

Lesson 5   Introductions to the IMO and China MSA
第 5 课   介绍国际海事组织和中国海事局

I . Introductions to the IMO

The IMO stands for the international maritime organization. Before May 22nd, 1982, the IMO was named IMCO which stands for the inter-governmental maritime consultative organization. It is the United Nations specialized agency with responsibility for the safety and security of shipping and the prevention of marine and atmospheric pollution by ships. IMO's work supports the UN sustainable development goals. The IMO was founded in 1959 as the IMO Convention was adopted in 1958.

1. Purposes and Missions of the IMO

The purposes of the Organization, as summarized by Article 1(a) of the Convention, are "to provide machinery for cooperation among Governments in the field of governmental regulation and practices relating to technical matters of all kinds affecting shipping engaged in international trade; to encourage and facilitate the general adoption of the highest practicable standards in matters concerning maritime safety, efficiency of navigation and prevention and control of marine pollution from ships". The Organization is also empowered to deal with administrative and legal matters related to these purposes.

The mission of the Organization as a United Nations specialized agency is to promote safe, secure, environmentally sound, efficient and sustainable shipping through cooperation. This will be accomplished by adopting the highest practicable standards of maritime safety and security, efficiency of navigation and prevention and control of pollution from ships, as well as through consideration of the related legal matters and effective implementation of IMO's instruments with a view to their universal and uniform application.

2. Structures of the IMO

2.1   Assembly

Assembly is the highest Governing Body of the Organization. It consists of all Member States and it meets once every two years in regular sessions, but may also meet in an extraordinary session if necessary. The Assembly is responsible for approving the work programme, voting on the budget and determining the financial arrangements of the Organization. The Assembly also elects the Council.

2.2 Council

The Council is elected by the Assembly for two-year terms beginning after each regular session of the Assembly. The Council is the Executive Organ of IMO and is responsible, under the Assembly, for supervising the work of the Organization. Between sessions of the Assembly, the Council performs all the functions of the Assembly, except the function of making recommendations to Governments on maritime safety and pollution prevention which is reserved for the Assembly by Article 15(j) of the Convention.

2.3 Maritime Safety Committee (MSC)

The MSC is the highest technical body of the Organization. It consists of all Member States. The functions of the Maritime Safety Committee are to "consider any matter within the scope of the Organization concerned with aids to navigation, construction and equipment of vessels, manning from a safety standpoint, rules for the prevention of collisions, handling of dangerous cargoes, maritime safety procedures and requirements, hydrographic information, log-books and navigational records, marine casualty investigations, salvage and rescue and any other matters directly affecting maritime safety".

The Committee is also required to provide machinery for performing any duties assigned to it by the IMO Convention or any duty within its scope of work which may be assigned to it by or under any international instrument and accepted by the Organization. It also has the responsibility for considering and submitting recommendations and guidelines on safety for possible adoption by the Assembly.

2.4 Marine Environment Protection Committee (MEPC)

The MEPC, which consists of all Member States, is empowered to consider any matter within the scope of the Organization concerned with prevention and control of pollution from ships. In particular, it is concerned with the adoption and amendment of conventions and other regulations and measures to ensure their enforcement.

The MEPC was first established as a subsidiary body of the Assembly and raised to full constitutional status in 1985.

2.5 Sub-Committees

The MSC and the MEPC are assisted in their work by a number of sub-committees which are also open to all Member States:

Sub-Committee on Human Element, Training and Watchkeeping (HTW);

Sub-Committee on Implementation of IMO Instruments (III);

Sub-Committee on Navigation, Communications and Search and Rescue (NCSR);

Sub-Committee on Pollution Prevention and Response (PPR);

Sub-Committee on Ship Design and Construction (SDC);

Sub-Committee on Ship Systems and Equipment (SSE); and

Sub-Committee on Carriage of Cargoes and Containers (CCC).

2.6 Legal Committee

The Legal Committee is empowered to deal with any legal matters within the scope of the Organization. The Committee consists of all Member States of IMO. It was established in 1967 as a subsidiary body to deal with legal questions which arose in the aftermath of the Torrey Canyon disaster.

The Legal Committee is also empowered to perform any duties within its scope which may be assigned by or under any other international instrument and accepted by the Organization.

2.7 Technical Cooperation Committee

The Technical Cooperation Committee is required to consider any matter within the scope of the Organization concerned with the implementation of technical cooperation projects for which the Organization acts as the executing or cooperating agency and any other matters related to the Organization's activities in the technical cooperation field.

The Technical Cooperation Committee consists of all Member States of IMO, was established in 1969 as a subsidiary body of the Council, and was institutionalized by means of an amendment to the IMO Convention which entered into force in 1984.

2.8 Facilitation Committee

The Facilitation Committee was established as a subsidiary body of the Council in May 1972, and became fully institutionalized in December 2008 as a result of an amendment to the IMO Convention. It consists of all the Member States of the Organization and deals with IMO's work in eliminating unnecessary formalities and "red tape" in international shipping by implementing all aspects of the Convention on Facilitation of International Maritime Traffic 1965 and any matter within the scope of the Organization concerned with the facilitation of international maritime traffic. In particular in recent years the Committee's work, in accordance with the wishes of the Assembly, has been to ensure that the right balance is struck between maritime security and the facilitation of international maritime trade.

2.9 Secretariat

The Secretariat of IMO consists of the Secretary-General and some 300 international personnel based at the headquarters of the Organization in London.

The Secretary-General of the Organization is Mr. Arsenio Dominguez (Republic of Panama) who was appointed to the position with effect from January 1, 2024, for an initial four-year term. At its 31st session (November-December 2019), the Assembly approved the renewal of Mr. Kitack Lim's appointment for a second and final term of four years (January 1, 2020 to December 31, 2023).

II. Introductions to China MSA

Under the direction of the Ministry of Transport of the People's Republic of China, China MSA is the Administration of Maritime Safety. China MSA stands for the Maritime Safety Administration of China. The headquarters is in Beijing.

1. Services

In accordance with the Maritime Traffic Safety Law of the People's Republic of China, the Marine Environment Protection Law of the People's Republic of China, and other related laws and regulations, the Maritime Safety Administration of the People's Republic of China (China MSA), under the Ministry of Transport, is the competent authority to exercise the administration of shipping safety and maintain the national sovereignty. The main responsibilities include:

1) drafting and implementing national policies, laws and regulations and standards regarding waterborne traffic safety supervision, survey and registration of ships and offshore installations, ship pollution prevention, and aids to navigation;

2) supervising waterborne traffic safety and preventing pollution from ships; inspecting safety management system of shipping companies; investigating and handling waterborne traffic accidents, and ship pollution accidents; instructing the compensation for pollution damage by ships;

3) administrating the survey of ships and off-shore facilities; supervising the statutory survey and certification for ships and off-shore facilities; examining the qualifications of ship survey organizations and surveyors, supervising the representative offices of foreign ship survey organizations within China; conducting registration, certification, inspection and certificate endorsement of Chinese-flagged ships; supervising foreign-flagged ships' entry into and exit from Chinese ports and waters; conducting safety supervision of carriage of dangerous cargoes and other cargoes by ships;

4) administering seafarers and pilots' training, examination and certification; examining the qualification and quality system of training institutions for seafarers and pilots; managing of seafarers' passports;

5) supervising waterborne traffic order and navigation conditions; designating and supervising restricted areas, routes, traffic control zones, anchorages and safe operation zones; examining and approving safe berthing conditions and maritime engineering operations relating to the safety of navigation; conducting work on removal of wrecks and other navigational obstacles; and issuing navigation warnings and notices to mariners;

6) Managing the A to N, radio navigation and safety communication; managing hydrographical survey of ports and routes and navigational publications; organizing and coordinating maritime search and rescue operations;

7) implementing international maritime conventions; fulfilling obligations of flag State, port State and coastal State; conducting international cooperation and exchanges; and

8) other responsibilities authorized by the Ministry of Transport.

2. Offices in China MSA

The major offices include Seafarer Management Division, Policy and Legislation Division, Traffic Management Division, Ship Registry and Supervision Division, Dangerous Goods and Pollution Prevention Division, Safety Management Division, Navigation Service Division.

3. Sub-MSAs

The sub-MSAs include Shanghai MSA, Tianjin MSA, Liaoning MSA, Hebei MSA, Shandong MSA, Jiangsu MSA, Zhejiang MSA, Fujian MSA, Guangdong MSA, Shenzhen MSA, Guangxi MSA, Changjiang MSA, Heilongjiang MSA, Lianyungang MSA, Beihai (Bohai and Huanghai) Navigation Support Centre, Nanhai (South China Sea) Navigation Support Centre, Donghai (East China Sea) Navigation Support Centre, etc.

4. Special Administrative Regions

Hong Kong Special Administrative Region and Macau Special Administrative Region are two special regions in maritime management. The central people's government empowered the maritime safety managements to local governments on maritime safety management.

In Taiwan Province, the so-called "Maritime and Port Bureau" is responsible for maritime safety management in local waters of Taiwan Province of the People's Republic of China.

III. Related Culture Words and Technical Terms

Maritime Safety Administration (海事安全主管机关)—It is a competent authority to control, manage, and inspect the shipping industry under the maritime laws of the country and the international maritime conventions. In China, China MSA is the Administration.

Maritime Safety Management (海事安全管理)—It is maritime safety management on behalf of the industry rather than the government.

control (*v.n.*) (控制)—In general, controls are from the government level. Port State Controls and Flag State controls are typical examples.

survey (*n.*) (船舶检验)—The Classification Society or other ship class organization inspects the vessel.

IV. Exercises

1. Discuss with your classmates and answer the following questions.

1) Are functions of the IMO the same as the IMCO?

2) Describe the organizations in the IMO.

3) Can you describe the departments in China MSA?

4) How can you make differences among Chinese terms "中国海事局" "直属海事局" "地方海事局"?

5) Why is the Chinese term "中国海事局" interpreted into China MSA rather than MSA of China?

6) What are the service divisions of China MSA?

7) How important of the Party, Administration, Union, and League in China? Please explain the causes.

8) What is the difference between the term Administration and management? Why are the term maritime managements used for Hong Kong and Macau Special Administrative

Region and Taiwan Province?

9）Why is Changjiang MSA established in China?

10）Why is the term "division" used for department in China MSA?

2. Deep thinking.

1）What is the relationship between the IMO and China MSA?

2）How is the China MSA connected to the IMO?

3）What is the relationship between China MSA and MoT China?

4）What is the relationship between China MSA and Liaoning MSA?

5）What is the relationship among Liaoning MSA, Shandong MSA, Shanghai MSA, Guangdong MSA, and Shenzhen MSA?

6）What is the relationship between Lianyungang MSA and Nanjing MSA?

7）What the function of Changjiang MSA?

8）How will the terms the IMCO and the IMO be pronounced and why?

9）How will you keep One China Principle in the maritime Administration?

10）Explain the relationship between Liaoning MSA and Dalian MSA.

3. Translate the following sentences into English.

1）中国海事局是代表中国政府行使海事管理的主管机关。其总部设在北京,隶属于中华人民共和国交通运输部。

2）在中央人民政府授权下,香港特区政府组建了香港海事处,香港海事处对我国香港特别行政区水域有着海事执法权。

3）按照级别来看,广东海事局和辽宁海事局都是中国海事局的直属局,这些海事局对于分管水域内有着海事执法权。

4）国际海事组织是联合国的下属机构,主要协调与管理海事事务,其总部在伦敦。

5）中国海事局机关办公地点设在北京市建国门内大街 11 号,内设业务机构有政策法规处、通航管理处、船舶监督处、危管防污处、船舶检验管理处、船舶技术规范处、船员管理处、安全管理处、航海保障管理处、科技信息处、国际合作处、执法督察处(地方海事管理处)。

4. Translate the following sentences into Chinese.

1）The functions of the Traffic Management Division of China MSA include but are not limited to：

manage the traffic order and traffic environment；organise to carry out water legislations and traffic control；plan and manage the traffic fairways, the no-go areas, traffic control areas, anchorages, and safe operating areas；manage the salvage of wrecks and clearing of the fairway；manage the broadcast of navigational warnings.

2）Safety has been at the heart of all of the IMO's activities since the Organization was established in 1948. The regulatory framework is continuously evolving as gaps become apparent and as a result of the IMO's proactive work to anticipate changes needed to accommodate emerging technologies and innovation—a prominent example being the currently ongoing development of a goal-based Code for maritime autonomous surface ships

(MASS Code).

3) It has always been recognized that the best way of improving safety at sea is by developing international regulations that are followed by all shipping nations and from the mid-19th century onwards a number of such treaties were adopted. Several countries proposed that a permanent international body should be established to promote maritime safety more effectively, but it was not until the establishment of the United Nations itself that these hopes were realized. In 1948 an international conference in Geneva adopted a convention formally establishing the IMO (the original name was the Inter-Governmental Maritime Consultative Organization, or IMCO, but the name was changed in 1982 to IMO).

4) The purposes of the IMO are to provide machinery for cooperation among Governments in the field of governmental regulation and practices relating to technical matters of all kinds affecting shipping engaged in international trade; to encourage and facilitate the general adoption of the highest practicable standards in matters concerning maritime safety, efficiency of navigation and prevention and control of marine pollution from ships.

5) The IMO was also given the task of establishing a system for providing compensation to those who had suffered financially as a result of pollution. Two treaties were adopted, in 1969 and 1971, which enabled victims of oil pollution to obtain compensation much more simply and quickly than had been possible before. Both treaties were amended in 1992, and again in 2000, to increase the limits of compensation payable to victims of pollution. A number of other legal conventions have been developed since, most of which concern liability and compensation issues.

Lesson 6　Introductions to Different Types of
Maritime Inspections
第6课　介绍不同种类的海事检查

I. Concepts of Inspections

The inspection is an official visit to a building or organization, or maritime unit to check that everything is satisfactory and that rules are being obeyed. The word inspection can be substituted by examination, check, appraisal, evaluation, test, or other terms. The inspection practice joins the blame culture.

The quarantine inspection, the customs inspection, and the immigration inspection are key procedures for foreign ships to visit a national port. For example, a Chinese ship shall pass through the quarantine and the customs inspection before arrival at a foreign port. The immigration inspection will be carried out during the entire laydays. In general, the quarantine inspection is the first inspection and the customs inspection will be the last inspection before departure from a foreign port.

II. Quarantine Inspection

Generally speaking, the quarantine inspection is the primary procedure for an incoming ship to visit a foreign port. The purpose of the quarantine inspection is to control the spreading of the infectious diseases possibly carried by the crewmembers or passengers on board ships. The Shipmaster or the Surgeon shall give evidence to show that all crewmembers and passengers are healthy and request free pratique. Any foreign ship on arrival or any national ship that visited foreign ports on the last voyage shall have a quarantine inspection before the transport service is completed. The quarantine inspection will be held at the anchorage or the berth, via radio pratique, or long quarantine inspection by Quarantine Officers on board, etc. The radio pratique is the quickest formality and the Shipmaster or the Agent will apply for free pratique if the ship is healthy. The Shipmaster or the surgeon shall fill up the Maritime Declaration of Health if the ship is healthy. It means that no infectious disease is found on board and the ship hasn't sailed to the epidemic area. Within 15 days, no fever case is found on board.

If any of the following cases is found, the quarantine inspection will be strictly carried out. The last port of call was an epidemic area or the ship arrived in an epidemic port within 15 days. The crewmember or passenger has contracted an infectious disease or has contacted the infectious disease patient. The infectious virus was found on board during quarantine inspection. Cargoes or articles are suspected to contain infectious diseases. Animals or plants with verminates are found on board. A crewmember or passenger is dead or is suspected of death on board. A corpse is found on board. A ship's sanitary condition is very severe.

In China, the quarantine inspection is performed by the customs officers, as the quarantine service is merged into General Administration of Customs of the People's Republic of China.

III. Customs Inspection

A customs inspection is significant during the entire laydays of a foreign ship. For a national ship, the customs inspection shall be carried out if the last port of call was a foreign port or the customs inspection shall be carried out if the national ship will sail to a foreign port. The purpose of a customs inspection is to prevent the smuggling. While the ship is on arrival, the Customs Officers will embark and seal the bonded store. The ship shall present several documents. For example, the Shipmaster or the Agent will submit the following documents: one copy of the entry report, two copies of the import cargo manifest, one copy of the list of passengers (if passengers are carried), one copy of crew lists, one copy of the list of crew's alcohol and cigarettes for personal use, a copy of the guarantee to obey the customs rule. In general, the Shipmaster shall sign all paper documents. If it is an e-version, an electronic signature shall be used. If a foreign ship is ready to depart from the port, the port shall pass a legal document (port clearance) to show that the ship is clear from the port. The next port of call will ask for the last port clearance to show that the ship was innocent in the last port of call and there was no violation in the last port of call.

IV. Immigration Inspection

An immigration inspection is an approach to prevent stowaways on board. An immigration inspection is carried out by the Immigration Officers. The Immigration Officers from the immigration office or the immigration bureau are to inspect all ships on arrival. During the inspection or before the inspection, the Shipmaster or the Agent shall show the Crew List and Passenger List to the immigration office. The Immigration Officer may board the ship to physically verify all crewmembers and passengers in conformity with the list of crewmembers and passengers. One way to control the stowaways is to issue shore passes for all crewmembers on board. Prior to mooring, the Shipmaster or the Agent will send the list of crewmembers to the Immigration Officers. The Immigration Officers will issue them with shore passes. The shore passes are only valid in the laydays. The shore passes are required to return to the Customs Officers prior to departure.

V. Other Inspections

1. Flag State Control

The FSC stands for flag state control which is a term to describe that a commercial ship is registered or licensed under the maritime rules, codes, or laws of the country.

The flag state implementation or the Administration has the authority to enforce regulations over vessels registered under her flag, including those relating to inspection, certification, and issuance of safety and pollution prevention documents. For instance, China MSA inspects Training Ship *Yukun* under FSC rules because Training Ship *Yukun* is a ship registered in China.

2. Port State Control

The PSC stands for port state control. It is an action that a PSCO checks a foreign ship in the port. If any deficiency is found, the PSCO may take action by drawing a warning letter, informing the classification society, informing the flag state, informing the Shipowner, forcing to rectify the deficiency on spot, or prior to the departure, or upon the arrival of the next port, or within 3 months, detaining the ship, forcing the ship to the shipyard for repair, etc.

3. Shipowner Inspection

In general, the Shipowner may send a Superintendent (short for SI) or the Designated Person Ashore (short for DPA) to board the ship while the ship gets alongside. The SI or DPA will seek for the deficiencies. If any deficiency is found, the Shipowner may take measures to punish the Shipmaster or responsible crewmembers.

4. Class Surveys

A class survey is the inspection carried out by the ship surveyors from the classification society. In contrast with other inspections, the class survey is generous. They care about the ship rather than punish her. The class survey includes the initial survey, the annual survey, the intermediate survey, the damage survey, the additional survey, and the renewal survey.

VI. Related Culture Words and Technical Terms

intervention (*n.*) (干涉,干预,介入)—Interfering or becoming involved, e. g. to prevent something from happening.

interfere (*v.*) (干涉,介入,干预)—Concern oneself with or take action affecting somebody else's affairs without the right to do something or being invited to do so. Interfere with something; handle, adjust, etc. something without permission, especially to cause damage.

scrutinize (*v.*) (仔细检查或者彻底检查)—Look at or examine something carefully or thoroughly.

surveillance (*n.*) (监视)—The careful watching kept on somebody suspected for doing wrong.

monitor (*v.*) (监听,监视)—Make continuous observation of something.

inspect （*v.*）（检查）—Examine closely.

examine （*v.*）（仔细观察,调查,检查）—Look at carefully in order to learn about or from; inspect closely.

test （*v.n.*）（测验,试验,考验）—Examine; examination or trial of the qualities, etc. of a person or thing.

smuggle （*v.*）（走私）—Get goods secretly and illegally into or out of a country, especially without paying customs duty.

layday （*n.*）（停泊期间,装卸货期间）—While a ship stays in port for cargo handling, the berthing time is called the layday.

stowaway （*n.*）（偷渡）—Hide himself or herself. They are also deemed as "stateless" In general, the stowaway hides himself or herself on board in order to bound for another place.

free pratique requirement （免检请求）—If the ship is healthy, the Shipmaster may ask for free pratique. In general, quarantine officers will not check the ship thoroughly if they agree on free pratique.

triple inspection （三方检查）or joint inspection （联合检查）—This style of inspection was used during the 1980s and 1990s in China. The quarantine inspection, maritime safety inspection, and customs inspection work together in order to make it convenience for ships.

coast guard inspection （海岸警卫队检查）—In some countries, the coast guard is the only organization to arrange all types of maritime inspections. U. S. C. G. is the typical example. The coast guard can be a type of inspection culture.

sea police or marine police （海警）—In many countries, sea police or marine police are employed to keep the public safety and security at sea.

radio pratique （无线电申请免检）—The radio pratique is the application by radio to indicate that the ship is healthy and request free pratique.

VII. Exercises

1. Discuss with your classmates and answer the following questions.

1）Which authority is responsible for customs inspections and quarantine inspections in China?

2）Can you make differences between the PSC and the FSC?

3）What department is responsible for the prevention of stowaways in China?

4）What are the PSC and the FSC?

5）What is the purpose of the immigration inspection?

6）What is the purpose of the customs inspection?

7）What is the purpose for quarantine inspection?

8）How can we find out rules for customs in China?

9）What is the coast guard established in many countries?

10）What is the bonded store （保税库,烟酒库） used for?

2. Deep thinking.

1）Why does the European Maritime Safety Agency（EMSA）particularly focus on marine pollution?

2）Why does China MSA focus on the safety of life at sea on the top?

3）If a stowaway is found on board a ship, what will the ship do?

4）While a ship is on berth, what inspections will she receive? Please list some.

5）Where can you find out the list of infectious diseases?

6）What may happen if a shipboard fails to make an entry formality before arrival?

7）In common practice, what will be the first check items before arrival at a foreign port and what will be the last check item before departure from a foreign port? What are the causes?

8）Please list some infectious diseases and where can we find out those?

9）What is the Maritime Declaration of Health?

10）Why do Customs Officers seal the bonded store while the ship is at the berth?

3. Translate the following sentences into English.

1）船旗国检查是对那些在本国注册的船舶的安全检查,而港口国检查是对进入本国的外轮的检查。

2）海关检查是专门检查船舶或者船上人员是否有走私贩私行为,一旦发现船舶或者船员有走私贩私行为,视其情节给予相应的处罚。

3）检疫检查是一个国家重要的防线,检疫主要针对从疫区归来的本国船只,或者从境外驶来的外籍船只。如果在本国第一个港口检查通过后,通常第二个挂靠港口不再进行检疫检查。

4）船东检查是船舶所有人对船舶进行的检查,检查涉及的船舶和船上人员的各个方面,船东检查必须坚持不懈,才能保证船舶安全事故降低至最低。

5）每个国家都有自己的主管移民机构,这些机构对于打击偷渡起到了重要作用,一旦发现偷渡者,通常需要将其遣返。

4. Translate the following sentences into Chinese.

1）When anyone asks me how I can best my experiences of nearly forty years at sea I merely say uneventful. Of course, there have been Winter gales and storms and fog and the like, but in all my experience I have never been in an accident of any sort worth speaking about. I have seen but one vessel in distress in all my years at sea, a brig, the crew of which was taken off in a small boat in charge of my Third Officer. I never saw a wreck and have never been wrecked, nor was I ever in any predicament that threatened to end in disaster of any sort.

2）The PSCO should also check that all relevant ISM Code documentation is on board. In particular, the PSCO should make random checks/use professional judgement to ensure that relevant functional requirements of the company's safety management system are documented and that relevant ship's staff are aware of their responsibilities and duties, in accordance with the ship's documented procedures and instructions.

3) During a detailed inspection, the PSCO will perform a more comprehensive review of the ISM Code documentation and check to ensure that the documented procedures are in place and are being properly implemented. The PSCO should verify compliance with a sufficient number of the following items during the detailed inspection. This may be done by interviewing relevant ship personnel, having the crew perform relevant tasks or drills, and examination of the relevant documents.

4) Is the company safety and environmental protection policy in place and are the crew familiar with it? The items may include the provision of safe practices in ship operations, safety assessment done and risks identified, safeguards against all identified risks, provision of a safe working environment, means for continuously improving crew's safety management skills and preparation for the safety and pollution emergencies, compliance with mandatory rules and regulations, account taken of applicable codes, guidelines, and standards.

5) Possible major non-conformities include: lack of a safe working environment, lack of safeguards against identified risks, lack of compliance with rules and regulations and account not being taken of applicable codes guidelines and recommendations by the IMO, the Administration, classification society and the maritime industry, lack of appropriate instructions and procedures, lack of adequate lines of communication.

Lesson 7   Management of Certificates and Documents
第 7 课   船舶、船员证书与文件管理

Certificates are official documents to show the party being certified meets the requirements of a law, rule, or convention. In a certificate, three important items will be read, namely the issuing party, the party being issued, the standard.

I . Ship Certificates

1. Class Certificates

Under the SOLAS 1974, MARPOL 73/78, LL 1966, and TC 1969, the class certificates are issued by the Classification Societies. Examples are International Loadline Certificate, International Tonnage Certificates, Cargo Ship Safety Construction Certificate, Cargo Ship Safety Radio Certificate, Cargo Ship Safety Equipment Certificate, etc. The Shipmaster or the nominee assigned by the Shipmaster is responsible for retaining those certificates in a safe locker. In general, certificates will be in valid within 5 years. Certificates will be checked during controls or inspections.

2. National Certificate and Statutory Certificate

A National Certificate is a certificate to show the relationship between the Administration and the Management Company. It decides the flag hoisted at the stern of the ship. For example, Training Ship *Yukun* is registered in China, so her nationality is the People's Republic of China.

Statutory Certificate, as the name suggests, is a legal certificate issued by the Administration or the classification society. Examples are the deratting or the deratting exemption certificate, the minimum safe manning certificate, the SOPEP, the fire-fighting equipment test certificate, the fire main test certificate, the calibration certificate, etc.

3. Exclusive Certificates

For some special types of ships, special certificates are required. For examples , special certificates are required for chemical ships , VLCCs , ULCCs , LNGs , LPGs , ro-ro passenger ships, MODU, etc.

II . Certificates for Crewmembers

Certificates for the Shipmaster or a particular crewmember are significant since certificates are evidences to show the Shipmaster or the crewmember is competent to work on board. While crewmembers work on board a ship, the Shipmaster or the nominee assigned by the Shipmaster is responsible for retaining certificates.

1. Certificate of Competency

The Certificate of Competency (CoC) is a certificate issued by the Administration to a crewmember to show the person is competent in relevant aspects of the STCW Convention. The CoC is merely issued for the Shipmaster or the Senior Officer under the standard of national laws in consultation with the STCW.

2. Basic Training Certificates (ZXX Code)

Basic Training Certificates, as the name suggests, are the certificates that all crewmembers shall be fitted with. In addition to the senior staff, all ratings shall hold the basic certificate. Depending upon the types of ships and trade areas, and/or positions on board, these certificates include the following:

Z01—Training Certificate for Familiarization and Basic Safety Training;

Z02—Training Certificate for Proficiency in Survival Crafts and Rescue Boats;

Z03—Training Certificate for Proficiency in Fast Rescue Boats;

Z04—Training Certificate for Advanced Fire-fighting Training;

Z05—Training Certificate for Proficiency in Medical First Aid;

Z06—Training Certificate for Medical Care on Board;

Z07—Training Certificate for Security Awareness on Board;

Z08—Training Certificate for Staff with Security Responsibility on Board;

Z09—Training Certificate for Ship Security Officer Training.

3. Special Training Certificates (TXX Code)

While a Shipmaster or a particular crewmember intends to work on a special ship, such as an oil tanker, a chemical ship, a high-speed vessel, a passenger ship, he or she shall have the associated special training certificates. Those certificates include:

T01—Basic Training Certificate for Operation of Oil and Chemical Tankers;

T02—Advanced Training Certificate for Cargo Operation of Oil Tankers;

T03—Advanced Training Certificate for Cargo Operation of Chemical Ships;

T04—Basic Training Certificate for Cargo Operation of Liquefied Ships;

T05—Advanced Training Certificate for Cargo Operation of Liquefied Ships;

T06—Special Training Certificate for Passenger Ships;

T07—Special Training Certificate for Manoeuvring of Large Ships;

T08—Special Training Certificate for High-speed Vessels;

T09—Special Training Certificate for Cargo Handling on Ships Carrying Dangerous and Hazardous Substance in Solid Form in Bulk;

T10—Special Training Certificate for Cargo Handling on Ships Carrying Dangerous and Hazardous Substance in Package Form.

4. Other Documents

The Seafarer's Passport is a book to show the personal identity of a crewmember. It may be used while the crewmember wants to enter the port after touring outside. It is a passport but used in the maritime field. A passport is a personal identity issued by the Public Security Authority in China to prove the identity of a particular person. A passport is used for the application of visas. A passport is the identity for use overseas. In short, a seafarer's passport and/or a passport is/are useful to prove the personal identity while questioned by a policeman, passing the customs office, or entering the port.

A Bill of Health is a document to show the holder is healthy. The Quarantine Officer gives the relevant person the document to show he or she is healthy. An inoculation paper is a document to show the injection history of anti-infectious diseases, such as yellow fever, cholera, plague, etc. During quarantine inspection, the Quarantine Officer will definitely check these Certificates.

5. Crew Mandatory Training and Certificate Renewal

The applicants need to attend mandatory training to get the certificates as per the relevant codes. The training centres have been assessed and approved by China MSA. The learning is arranged in classroom teaching. So far, there is no online training in order to guarantee the effectiveness of the training. All trainees shall attend the classes. Examinations or assessments will be arranged for those trainees before they are eligible to get the certificates.

In accordance with the STCW Convention, the CoCs will be valid only if the holders work on board ships for definite periods of time. In general, the holders will work on board for 12 months at the minimum. Otherwise, the CoCs will not be valid. However, some holders will keep the certificates up-to-date in terms of certificate renewal. The simulator training and mandatory training are effective to have the certificate renewed.

III. Related Culture Words and Technical Terms

ship papers (船舶文件)—Books and documents required to be held by a ship. Include Certificate of Registry, Articles of Agreement, official logbook, bill of health, free board certificate, radio certificate and document related to cargo.

ship's husband (船舶管理者)—A person formerly carried in a merchant ship to transact ship's business and purchase stores. In earlier times, was the boatswain, and was in charge of the crew and of the fabric of the ship.

certificate folio (证书夹)—In general, ship's certificates are stowed and managed in a folio. The category covers the package.

validity of certificate (证书有效性)—In common practice, a certificate will be valid within 5 years. The certificate is still effective within the valid period.

expiry date (过期日)—A certificate will expire after the expiry date. The expiry date is just the day to show whether the certificate is effective or not.

unseaworthiness (*n.*) (不适航性)—The ship is unfit to go to sea. The unfitness may be caused by the defective condition of the ship's hull, machinery, or equipment. The unseaworthiness may also be caused by overloading or improper loading. The Shipmaster and the owner will have valid defence if they can prove that they had made arrangements to restore the vessel's fitness before going to sea or that it was reasonable not to have made such arrangements to guarantee that the ship is seaworthy.

certificate and certification（证书与发证）—A certificate is a legal document to show the holder or the entity is in compliance with the convention, law, code, and rules. A certification is an action to certify a document for a holder or an entity.

Ⅳ. Exercises

1. Discuss with your classmates and answer the following questions.

1）What does the abbreviation CoC stand for?

2）What is the difference between a basic training certificate and a special training certificate?

3）Who manages the certificate on board the ship?

4）What is the difference between a ship certificate and a personal certificate?

5）What is the difference between the seafarer's passport and the national passport?

6）In China, who issues the national passport for Chinese citizens?

7）What is called "visa"?

8）Why does a country check the visa while the foreigners port the entry?

9）By what convention, a CoC is issued?

10）What does the term certificate renewal mean?

2. Deep thinking.

1）If a Shipmaster wants to work on board an oil tanker, what certificate must he or she hold for competence?

2）If a sailor wants to work on board an oil tanker, what certificate must he or she hold for the competence?

3）What does a certificate of competence mean?

4）If a CoC is missing, what will the holder do?

5）If a crewmember's passport is missing, what will the crewmember do?

6）Some countries require the crewmembers to hold transit visas. Why do they ask for those visas?

7）What is the difference between the Prize Certificate (or a Honour Certificate) and a Driver's License.

8）A staff from the management company says CoCs should be managed by the company. Crewmembers don't have the right to carry that personally. What is your opinion on that point of view?

9）What is the standard for issuing a CoC in China?

10）What are the roles of an official seal and signature in the certificate?

3. Translate the following sentences into English.

1）船舶证书是由主管机关或者船级社发给船舶的官方文件，显示根据某个国际海事公约或者国内法规，该船某个方面达到了要求。

2）"船员服务簿"是船员在船司职证明的法定文书，通常包括船员姓名、司职的船名、上下船地点、船舶总吨、主推进功率、船员签名、船章、船长签名等。

3）"四小证"是指上船工作最基本安全证书，因为最初有四个而得名。证书包括《基本安全培训证书》《精通救生艇筏和救助艇培训合格证》《高级消防培训合格证》《精通急救培训合格证》。

4）"大证"系指船员上船司职的职务证书，由于在《1978 年海员培训、发证和值班标准国际公约》的履约阶段，当时的中国港监（现名中国海事局）颁发的证书比"四小证"大，因此俗称"大证"。

5）如果某船的"安全管理证书"被吊销，那么由于该船的重大不符合很有可能导致"公司安全管理体系"存在着严重的缺陷，而导致公司的"符合证明"的正本证书被吊销，企业不得不重新进行管理体系的审核申请。

4. Translate the following sentences into Chinese.

1）The following form of supplement is added to the existing form：

Supplement to the cargo ship safety construction certificate. It is signed by the country with official seal. The content includes name of ship, distinctive number or letters, port of registry, deadweight of ship in metric tons, year of build.

2）This is to certify that the ship has been surveyed in accordance with Regulation 10 of Chapter Ⅰ of the Protocol of 1978 Relating to the International Convention for the Safety of Life at Sea, 1974; and that the survey showed that the condition of the hull, machinery and equipment as defined in the above Regulation was in all respects satisfactory and that the ship complied with the requirement of that Protocol.

3）This is to certify that, at an annual/intermediate survey in accordance with regulation 1/14（h）（iii）of the Convention, the ship was found to comply with the relevant requirement of the Convention. The certificate will be signed in the signature of the authorized official in a designated place in the definite time.

4）In a particular ship, the details of life-saving appliances include total number of lifeboats, total number of persons accommodated by the lifeboats, number of self-righting partially enclosed lifeboats, number of totally enclosed lifeboats, number of lifeboats with a self-contained air support system, number of fire-protected lifeboats, number of rescue boats, number of liferafts, number of lifebuoys, number of lifejackets, number of immersion suits.

5）A seaman includes every person（except Shipmasters and Pilots）employed or engaged in any capacity on board any ship. Ships' Officers are therefore classed as seamen: for welfare purposes, the Shipmaster is usually included in this category. As in the past, only persons aged 18 or over can be employed on board a ship, though in certain capacities persons between the ages of 16-18 can also be engaged.

Chapter Three
Culture on Shipping Economy

第三章
航运经济文化

本章学习目的及本章内容提要

  通过本章学习了解国际航运现状和中国航运现状，了解全球航运指数和国内航运指数的区别与联系。了解国家主席习近平提出的"一带一路"重大倡议和中国国内航运指数乃至世界航运经济的联系。掌握船舶代理及船舶货运代理的操作流程，船舶代理和货运代理中的重要术语。

Lesson 8   Introductions to World and
Domestic Shipping Indices
第 8 课   国际和国内航运指数介绍

The transport index is used to value the status of the transport.

I . World Indices for Shipping

Those indices have being used for centuries in the world to indicate the status of the world wide transportation.

1. Baltic Dry Index (BDI)

The Baltic Dry Index (BDI) is issued daily by the London-based Baltic Exchange. It is the indicator for dry cargo transportation. The BDI is a composite of the Capesize, Panamax and Supramax Time charter Averages. It is reported around the world as a proxy for dry bulk shipping stocks as well as a general shipping market bellwether.

The BDI is the successor to the Baltic Freight Index (BFI) and came into operation on 1st November, 1999. The BDI continues the established time series of the BFI, however, the voyages and vessels covered by the index have changed over time, so caution should be exercised in assuming long term constancy of the data.

In 1744, the Virginia and Maryland coffee house in Threadneedle Street, London, changed its name to Virginia and Baltick, to more accurately describe the business interests of the merchants who gathered there. Today's Baltic Exchange has its roots in a committee of merchants formed in 1823 to regulate trading and formalize the exchange of securities on the premises, which by then had moved to the Antwerp Tavern. The first daily freight index was published by the Baltic Exchange in January 1985.

2. Baltic Dirty Tank (BDTI) and Baltic Clean Tank Index (BCTI)

BDTI stands for Baltic Dirty Tank Index and BCTI means Baltic Clean Tank Index. They are the indicators for liquid bulk cargo transportation. Dirty and clean in the BDTI and BCTI are metaphors to refer to the crude oil and product oil respectively, as the crude oil is impure (In other word, it is dirty.) and the product oil is comparatively pure (In other word, it is clean.). The types of oil tankers include crude oil carriers and product oil tankers dependent upon the cargo. The classification of BDTI and BCTI is in this approach. Providing that the classification is on the basis of sizes, the tankers include ULCC, VLCC, Suezmax, Aframax, Panamax, and Handy. The deadweight tons of BDTI tankers are much larger than those of BCTI tankers. The ULCC stands for Ultra large Crude Carrier and the deadweight tons of ULCC are more than 320 000. The VLCC stands for Very Large Crude Carriers and the deadweight tons may range from 200, 000 to 320, 000. Suezmax , as the name recommends , is the largest oil tanker which can transit Suez Canal. In general, the deadweight tons are between 120,000 and 200,000. Aframax means the maximum ship of Average Freight Rate Assessment, is a type of ship which can travel most areas, including small gulfs , icy waters, etc. The deadweight tons range from 85,000 to 120,000. Panamax refers to the maximum oil tanker which can transit Panama Canal. The deadweight tons are from 60,000 to 85,000. The deadweight tons of other oil tankers are below 60,000.

3. HARPEX Shipping Index and World Container Index (WCI)

HARPEX Shipping Index is the container index that the container ship index of ship brokers Harper Petersen & Co. The HARPEX Shipping Index tracks weekly container shipping rate changes in the time charter market for eight classes of all-container ships. The index was compiled in 2004, but by using a database of 10,000 records, can be calculated retrospectively back to 1986. The HARPEX Shipping Index is considered a suitable indicator of global economic fleet shipping activity since it tracks changes in freight rates for container ships over broad categories. This index is slightly different from the better-known Baltic Dry Index that tracks freight costs for dry bulk ships that usually carry bulk cargoes and raw materials such as coal, ore and grain.

The World Container Index (WCI) assessed by Drewry is a composite of container freight rates on 8 major routes to/from the US, Europe. It is the indicator to show the boom or bust in the international container market. It plays less important role in the world transportation market, as it merely takes 15% of the world transportation market. However, it is predicted that the container transportation will be increased significantly in the near future, as it is a tendency that general cargo will be containerized in the world market.

II. Domestic Indices

China is the second largest economy in the world. The transport plays a significant role in the world transportation. It is necessary to calculate the indices under the influence of China, especially after the BRI cooperation.

1. Belt and Road Shipping and Trade Index (BRSTI)

The Belt and Road Shipping and Trade Index (BRSTI) is to show the achievement of BRI on smooth trade and transportation. Shanghai Shipping Exchange (SSE) researched and developed the Silk Road Freight and Trade Index (SRFTI) and Maritime Silk Road Freight Index (MFSI). Shanghai Shipping Exchange officially published BRSTI in July, 2017. It consists of the Belt and Road Trade Value Index (BRTVI), Belt and Road Cargo Volume Index (BRCVI), and Maritime Silk Road Freight Index (SRFI).

2. China (Export) Containerized Freight Index (CCFI)

China (Export) Containerized Freight Index (CCFI) sponsored by the Ministry of Transport and formulated by Shanghai Shipping Exchange was firstly published on 13th

April, 1998. It is the indicator to show the container transportation relating to China.

3. Export Containerized Freight Index (SCFI)

For the purpose of satisfying the demand of developing international container freight derivatives and improving the system of China's export containerized freight indices, Shanghai Export Containerized Freight Index (SCFI) was officially launched as of 16th October, 2009.

4. China Coastal Bulk Freight Index (CBFI)

To fully reflecting the fluctuation of Chinese coastal transport market, Shanghai Shipping Exchange officially initiated China Coastal Bulk Freight Index (CBFI) on 28th November 2001 under the guidance of the Ministry of Transport of the People's Republic of China. This new tool also better displays the market situation during the period of waterway transport pricing system reform, and boost the sound development of China Coastal Shipping market.

5. China (Coastal) Bulk Coal Freight Index (CBCFI)

For the purpose of timely reflecting the frequent and drastic fluctuation of freight rates of China's coastal coal transport market, and implementing the instructions of the State Council in the Opinions on Building "Two Centres" in Shanghai, "... to enrich shipping finance product lines, speed up development of shipping freight index derivatives and create favorable conditions for Chinese shipping enterprises to control transport risks...", Shanghai Shipping Exchange has, on the basis of existing system of China (Coastal) Bulk Freight Index (CBFI), developed the China (Coastal) Bulk Coal Freight Index (CBCFI) and publicizes the composite index and spot rates for different routes/types of vessels of coastal coal service market every day.

6. Global Carrier Schedule Performance (GCSP)

As a "benchmark" for measuring the quality of carrier services, the schedule performance of carrier services has always been a long-term focus of marine operation stakeholders and related parties in shipping industry. In order to adapt to the changes in the container shipping market and high-quality service requirements, and to meet the individual needs of major shipping, trading, and logistics companies, Shanghai Shipping Exchange, together with CargoSmart Limited (CargoSmart), researched and developed the "Global Carrier Schedule Performance (GCSP)".

7. China Import Dry Bulk Freight Index (CDFI)

China has a great weight in global bulk shipping market. It has taken almost up to 50% share of global shipping in coal, ore and grain shipping sector. The "China influence" has become increasingly important to the market. In order to reveal the supply-demand situation of the international dry bulk shipping market, provide the right guidance reflecting international dry bulk shipping market conditions, and give the support for decision-making on the macro-controlling and business operating, Shanghai Shipping Exchange has developed China Import Dry Bulk Freight Index (CDFI) under the guidance of the Ministry of Transport of the People's Republic of China. After one year trail run, it was official launched in 28th November, 2013.

8. Far East Dry Bulk Index (FDI)

With the eastward shift of Asia Pacific to the global shipping center, the Far East has become more prominent in the global dry bulk trade. In order to better meet the needs of shipping business development in the Far East, the Shanghai Shipping Exchange imported dry bulk freight index. On the basis of further research and development of the Far East Dry Bulk Index (FDI), on November 28, 2017 officially released.

9. Crude Oil Tanker Freight Index (CTFI)

The crude oil is an important strategic material related to national economic lifelines. China is the world's second-largest oil consumer as well as the world's second-largest crude oil importer. It is very necessary and important to provide the weathervane for imported crude oil transportation market in China or even for Asia-Pacific region which can reflect changes and trends in the shipping market conditions. It is expected to offer the shipper and shipowner a derivative tool to circumvent the freight rate risk. Meanwhile, such product and movement will enhance the power of China to have the corresponding influence on the international crude oil trade and transportation business. Under the guidance of the Ministry of Transport, Shanghai Shipping Exchange (SSE), developed the China Import Crude Oil Tanker Freight Index (CTFI). The index was launched in November 28, 2013.

10. China Import Containerized Freight Index (CTCFI)

Since the adjustment and upgrade of industrial structure in China, the shift of export-oriented market for growth of China import volume, the improvement of bi-directional imbalance in liner transport, the change of China import containerized freight has been increasingly important for shipping and trading enterprises. For the purpose of meeting the demand of fast developing Chinese import container market, fully reflecting the market conditions of China foreign trade container transport, and perfecting China containerized freight index system, Shanghai Shipping Exchange (SSE) researched and developed China Import Containerized Freight Index (CICFI). The CICFI was officially published on November 30, 2015, including the composite index and 5 sub-indices for the sample routes.

On November 16, 2022 the new version of the CICFI is officially published, including the composite index and 12 sub-indices for the sample routes.

11. Southeast Asia Freight Index (SEAFI)

For the purpose of meeting the demand of timeliness, precision and sensitivity of freight rates in the Southeast Asia container shipping market, fully reflecting the market conditions in the area, and perfecting SCFI index serials, Shanghai Shipping Exchange (SSE) researched and developed Southeast Asia Freight Index (SEAFI), which began its external trial run from November 30, 2015.

12. China Crew's Remuneration Index (CCRI)

In order to further accelerate the supply-side reform of Chinese seafarers market, better safeguard the rights and interests of Chinese seafarers, promote and optimize the allocation of human resources in seafarers market, establish an efficient operation system of seafarers market, and support the healthy development of seafarers market, with the support of Shanghai Maritime Administration and the active efforts of all relevant parties, Shanghai Shipping Exchange has developed the China (Shanghai) Crew's Remuneration Index (CCRI) and started its trial operation on June 25, 2017.

Ⅲ. Related Culture Words and Technical Terms

economic indicator (经济晴雨表)—An economic indicator is a statistic about an economic activity. Economic indicators allow analysis of economic performance and predictions of future performance. One application of economic indicators is the study of business cycles. Economic indicators include various indices, earnings reports, and economic summaries: for example, the unemployment rate, quits rate (quit rate in American English), housing starts, consumer price index (a measure for inflation), consumer leverage ratio, industrial production, bankruptcies, gross domestic product, broadband internet penetration, retail sales, stock market prices, and money supply changes.

benchmark (*n.*) (基准)—Measurements and other evaluations. It is used to evaluate the activities in the shipping industry.

economy (*n.*) (经济体)—Operation and management of a country's money supply, trade and industry. It also refers to the economy body. For example, China is the second largest economy in the world.

maritime economics (海运经济学)—Maritime economics is a discipline or field of study connected with the manner in which existing material and human resources are used in the industry and how they change and develop over time. Maritime economic theory consists of a body of concepts and principles which assist in the explanation of the industry's progress.

shipping economics (航运经济学)—Shipping economics is concerned with the economics of transporting freight by ships.

ship economics (船舶经济学)—It is concerned with the economics of ships that are used in maritime transportation.

port economics (港口经济学)—It is concerned with the economics of ports, i.e., the provision of port services and the users of these services.

Ⅳ. Exercises

1. Discuss with your classmates and answer the following questions.

1) What does the BRI stand for?
2) What is the difference between the BRSTI and the BDI?
3) What do the BDTI and the BCTI stand for?
4) Why do we use the term economy instead of economic body?
5) What is the technical term for costal bulk freight index in China?

6) Which organization creates shipping indices for the BRI?

7) What is the difference between the MoT of the People's Republic of China and the MoC of the People's Republic of China?

8) What does the GCSP stand for?

9) What does the CTCFI stand for?

10) When was the BRSTI firstly launched?

2. Deep thinking.

1) Why is the BRI well welcomed by all peoples?

2) Why is the maritime economics different from economics?

3) In China, it is quite popular to treat someone's a banquet. In western countries, it is also popular to treat other's coffee. What is the cause of the culture behind?

4) Where is the Far East? Please tell us the standpoint who used the term?

5) Tell us the importance to achieve the transportation prosperity inrealising the Chinese Dream of national rejuvenation.

6) Compare Aframax, Suezmax, Panamax, and Malaccamax and explain the word structure of those words.

7) Why is it important to develop the BRI indices?

8) Compare Harpex with the SCFI.

9) Can you give examples on eastward shift of world shipping?

10) What does it mean when the BDI is falling down?

3. Translate the following sentences into English.

1)"一带一路"航运指数是对"一带一路"航运活动衡量高低走势的体现,能够实时地反映出"一带一路"建设国参与"一带一路"航运建设的具体情况。

2)"一带一路"是"丝绸之路经济带"和"21世纪海上丝绸之路"的简称。2013年9月和10月由中国国家主席习近平分别提出。依靠中国与有关国家既有的双边或者多边机制,借助既有的、行之有效的区域合作平台,借用古代丝绸之路的文化符号,用和平发展的理念,和沿线国家共同打造政治互信、经济融合、文化包容的利益共同体、命运共同体、责任共同体。

3)航运经济学是研究国际海上货物运输的学问,航运经济学被视为运输经济学的一部分,而运输经济学又是产业经济学的一部分,后者又是经济学的一个分支,属于微观经济学的范畴。

4)航运业遇到的问题通常是该行业所特有的,并可以运用对经济学原理或者经济学常识给予解释。

5)虽然航运经济学是运输经济学的组成部分,但是它与运输经济学依然存在明显的差别。两者不同之处在于,运输经济学通常只是研究一国或经济体内运输的学问,而航运经济学则是研究海上运输的学问。

4. Translate the following sentences into Chinese.

1) Every working day, a panel of international shipbrokers submits their assessment of the current freight cost on various routes to the Baltic Exchange. The routes are meant to be

representative, i. e. large enough in volume to matter for the overall market. These rate assessments are then weighted together to create both the overall BDI and the size specific Capesize, Panamax, and Supramax indices. The BDI factors in three different sizes of oceangoing dry bulk transport vessels:

2) The Baltic Dry Index (BDI), is issued daily by the London-based Baltic Exchange. The BDI is a composite of the Capesize, Panamax and Supramax Time Charter Averages. It is reported around the world as a proxy for dry bulk shipping stocks as well as a general shipping market bellwether. The BDI is the successor to the Baltic Freight Index (BFI) and came into operation on November 1, 1999. The BDI continues the established time series of the BFI, however, the voyages and vessels covered by the index have changed over time so caution should be exercised in assuming long term constancy of the data.

3) The BDTI stands for the Baltic Dirty Tank Index whereas the BCTI stands for the Baltic Clean Tank Index. Dirty and clean in the BDTI and the BCTI are metaphors which refer to the crude oil (dirty) and the product oil (clean) respectively. The crude oil tankers are very large in size. VLCCs and ULCCs are much larger than the product oil carriers.

4) The Harpex Shipping Index is the container index and the name was from the Harper-Petersen & Co. The Harpex Shipping Index tracks weekly container shipping rate changes in the time charter market for eight classes of all container ships. The index was originally compiled in 2004.

5) The Baltic Dry Index (BDI) is an economic indicator issued daily by the London-based Baltic Exchange. It just looks like Dow Jones, Heng Sheng, Nikkei, SSE (Shanghai Stock Exchange), New York, Stock Exchange Composite, indices in the stock markets. The word Baltic in the BDI does not narrowly refer to the Baltic Sea countries, but it has the historical background. It was originally traced back to 1744.

Lesson 9　Ship Agency and Cargo Agency
第 9 课　船舶代理和货运代理

Ⅰ. Ship Agency

1. Ship Agent and Agency

The ship agency is a service designated by the Consignor or Consignee, Shipowner, Ship Charterer and Ship Agent is a person who does agency. The agency provides all-round services for ships and the agency is unable to provide services directly and the agency will communicate with other parties in order to gain the services. For instances, the pilot station provides pilotage, but the Agent can communicate with the pilot station on behalf of the ship to get the pilotage; the port authority provides berth allocations for ships , but the Agent can communicate with the port to get the berths for ships on arrival; the Agent may communicate with customs office to submit all formalities before the ship arrives and the ship will be permitted to enter the port for cargo operation smoothly upon arrival, and so forth.

2. Types of Ship Agency and Agency in China

In China, most agencies are small and private, but there is only one large state-run ship agency in China—China Ocean Shipping Agency. It was founded on first of January 1953 and it was the leader of international shipping and transportation agency in China. The abbreviation is PENAVICO since it started from People's Navigation Company. The headquarters is located in Beijing and it has over 80 domestic port offices, more than 300 business stations and overseas representative offices in US, Europe countries, Japan, Republic of Korea, and Singapore.

Ship agency. The ship agency is the core service for the ship agency. It looks like a shore-based household for the ship.

Ship running agency. On the basis of the charter party, the agency is responsible for ship's running while the ship gets alongside.

Agency on behalf of charterer. The charterer may hire agency to protect the rights. Under the charter party, the Shipowner may order the Shipmaster to use the agency and pay for dues and agency fees in the port. Albeit the agency is the representative of the charterer, the agency is also responsible for the Shipowner under the charter party.

Agency for ship management. The agency is responsible for bunkering, ship repair, crewmember service on behalf of the Shipowner. The Shipowner may hire running operator to manage the ship. Parts of those agencies are crew management companies in China.

Agency for tramps or partial agency. In order to save money, the Shipowner may only empower some rights of Agent services to the agency in the port where the ship seldom calls at. While the agency performs the service, the agency may ask the Shipowner first.

3. Ship Agency Service

The ship agency service includes the following:

Prior to arrival, the ship Agent will do entry formalities in response to the requirements as per the national laws. The Agent will do customs, quarantine, immigration services on behalf of the Shipowner. The Agent will communicate with the pilot station to book pilotage service for the in-coming ship. The Agent will communicate with the port authority to book the berth for the represented ship. The Agent will communicate with the Shipowner to receive any orders from the Shipowner and the Agent will pass the orders to the Shipmaster while the Agent meets the Shipmaster. The Agent will communicate with the tug company in order to order tugs. The Agent will communicate with the stevedore company and tally agency for cargo handling work. If the cargo was damaged, the Agent may also call the Cargo Surveyor or the Lawyer for settling the reimbursement or hearing in a maritime court, etc. The Agent will also organize the purchases for replenishments, stores and spare parts for the represented ship. The Agent will do the departure formality for the ship, for instance, the customs, immigration, and maritime organizations will be informed and the port clearance will be applied for. The Agent shall be familiar with the other services. For instance, the Agent may arrange the city touring if the Shipmaster requires under the approval of the Shipowner. The Agent may arrange hospitalization if the crewmember was ill. The Agent may arrange any potential services if the Shipmaster asks. For example, the Agent may arrange lawyers to settle the hearing if any crewmember violated the local laws while he or she stayed on shore. If possible, the Agent may inform the persons in consulate or embassy of the nation which the violator is from.

4. Cargo Agency Service

In common practice, the cargo agency service is a part of ship agency. The cargo agency includes the payment of port dues, light dues, berth dues, and charges for cargo lashing and securing. Those businesses include two different types. One cargo agency is the service for the Shipowner. It is a part of ship agency. Another cargo agency is on behalf of cargo owner. In that case, the ship agency extends the service. It takes own risks to look for a right ship to carry the cargo for the cargo owner. The Shipowner may ask the freight and the cargo Agent may increase the profits and ask the cargo freight and the benefits from the cargo owner. The cargo agency may consider hiring the entire ship or holds on board to achieve the cargo transport business.

5. Ship Operation Service

In recent years, the ship agency includes the management of ships. The Shipowner may give the ship to the agency. The agency may employ the Shipmaster and crewmembers to serve on board a ship. The agency may use the peculiar safety management system to run the ship.

6. Disponent Owner

In recent years, one of the value-added services is the chartering. The agency may charter a ship to fulfill the voyage charter party or time charter party services. Voyage charter party refers to the hiring of a ship for merely one voyage whereas the time charter party means the employment of a ship in definite period of time. If a ship is hired, the Agent becomes a " Shipowner". The agency may act as the Shipowner in order to use the ship to earn the freights.

II. Maritime Logistics

Maritime logistics is a trade to serve cargo transport from end to end. The persons who do the maritime logistics are called operators.

1. Both Ends

If we want to comprehend this trade, we shall know the two ends on the logistic chain. One side is called Cargo Owner. The term Cargo Owner, as the name suggests, is the person or party who owns the cargo for sale. In foreign trade term, the Cargo Owner is the sender of the cargo. The cargo may be bought by a business dealer or a cargo transport operator. The other end is the cargo buyer. The cargo will be transported to the port which is designated by the cargo buyer. The very significant party between the seller and buyer is the transportation party. The transportation party is called cargo carrier. The term is a party who transports the cargo in order to earn the freight.

2. Cargo Operator or Broker

The Cargo Operator is a person who does the service in the logistic chain. The Cargo Broker is a person who does the "go-between" service between seller and buyer. They may care the transportation business. In contrast with the Cargo Broker, the Cargo Operator may take more risks, since they may buy the cargo from the real cargo owner and do the business with the buyer directly. Hence the Cargo Operator may make more money than the Broker as the Cargo Operator takes more risks. The Cargo Broker acts as a bridge between two ends and Cargo Operator acts as the seller and the bridge. A pure Cargo Broker can't do a successful international business, so most of them act as the Cargo Operator.

3. Maritime Logistic Business Procedures

There are different procedures in accordance with business types. For example, a buyer or a seller may look for ships for transportation. He or she may offer types of cargo, destination, requirements in transportation, time of departure, and time of arrival, etc. He or she may look for particular ship(s) for cargo transportation. They may negotiate on the freight and then they make contracts on the cargo transport. If a cargo operator owns ships, he or she may also purchase some cargoes and look for potential buyers.

4. Cargo Transportation Procedures

In general, the responsibilities for carriers include, cargo loading, discharging (unloading), cargo transportation , and cargo care. A cargo loading means the cargo is loading on board from the quay or other vessels. The cargo loading is operated in order to guarantee less cargo damage or cargo shortage, or even missing during the loading operation. Cargo unloading or discharging is a procedure to deliver the cargo to the shore-side or other designated ship or location. The significance in the cargo unloading is to avoid cargo damage, cargo shortage or missing, deliver to wrong person, etc. The cargo care is the carrier's responsibility during cargo transportation. For example, some cargoes need ventilation, and some cargoes need cooling, etc. The cargo transportation is a physical movement for the cargo from one place to another place by sea.

Prior to transportation, the Shipping Note and Shipping Order will be given to the carrying party and the ship. A Shipping Note (short as B/N, 下货纸) is a document to the Carrier as per the contract and it was made by the Shipper. The Shipping Order (short as S/O, 装货单) is a document to the ship for the carrying duty. It includes types and tonnage of the cargo. The Mate's Receipt (short as M/R, 大副收据) is a document to show the Carrier has well received the cargo on board after the cargo loading. It shows the care duty has been transferred to the Carrier. Stowage Plan (积载图) is a document made by the Chief Mate on board or other person as per the contract. The Stowage Plan is scientific as the ship's stability (G/M Value), stress distribution, and cargo compatibility should be considered in the Stowage Plan making. The Shipping List or the Loading List (short as L/L, 载货清单) is a document made for Agent used for port clearance. In other words, it is a document used for customs clearance to report to the local customs office in loading port to show the shipping operation is in compliance with national laws and international maritime conventions. Cargo Manifest is a list made by the Carrier or the Agent in accordance with the Stowage Plan. In general, this document is made by the Chief Mate and permitted by the Shipmaster.

In transportation, the Carrier shall make every endeavour to care the cargo in good condition. If the cargo was damaged or lost during transportation due to the stress of weather, the Shipmaster shall make a Sea Protest (海事声明) to state the damage or missing is the force majeure or act of God.

Prior to the delivery to the correct receiver, the Bill of Lading (short as B/L) was made by the Shipper or the Carrier. It will be mailed different from the ship. In general, the paper B/L will be in duplicate or triplicate. The Bill of Lading may be divided into two types, namely clean B/L and unclean B/L. If the cargo was damaged in the process of loading, the Chief Mate on board will sign the B/L to state the damaged cargo in order to avoid the responsibility for the damage. That Bill of Lading is called unclean B/L. If any copy of a Bill of Lading is used to claim the right of the cargo, the other Bill(s) of Lading is (are) in vain. In other words, that will be changed into the duplicate of B/L and the duplicate B/L can be used for other services instead. In other words, the duplication won't be applicable to the associate laws. While the original Bill of Lading is used for claiming the cargo, the carrier shall sign it, but the other duplicate Bill of Lading is in vain and the carrier will not sign the duplicate one (s).

III. Related Culture Words and Technical Terms

force majeure (天灾)—It is a French commercial term for unavoidable accidents in the transport of goods. It is also called act of God. It is frequently used in the Sea Protest or in the insurance.

shipper (*n.*) (装船人,海员的旧称)—One who puts goods into a ship for carriage. At one time the name was applied to a seaman.

bill of lading (提单)—Receipt given by the Shipmaster, or other representative of owner, to shipper of cargo when received on board. It not a contract of carriage but should epitomize the conditions under which the goods specified are carried.

Hague Rules,1921 (1921 年海牙规则)—Enunciated certain rules and conditions regarding the carriage of goods by sea; most of these rules being incorporated in the Carriage of Goods by Sea Act, 1924.

bill of store (物料清单)—Document authorizing shipment of dutiable articles as ship's stores and free of duty.

freight or freightage (运费)—Goods loaded for transport in a vessel. 2 Money paid for carriage of goods by sea. In marine insurance, includes value of service in carrying goods of owner. It does not include passage money.

general average (共同海损)—General indemnity made by all interests concerned—and in proportion to the financial value of property each had at stake—for a maritime loss deliberately but reasonably incurred for the safety of the remaining property when in peril.

particular average (单独海损)—Indemnity due from a particular person or persons to make good a particular maritime loss against which insurance had been effected.

hire and payment clause (租船和付款条款)—Inserted in a time charter to specify amount of money to be paid, and when payment is to be made.

insurance clubs (保险机构)—They are the small damage clubs or mutual indemnity associations.

insurer (*n.*) (投保人)—Person(s) who have contracted to make good a maritime loss.

home trade agreement (内贸协议)—Contract between master and crew of vessel in the home trade. In general, it is enforced for six months from date of opening. Wages are usually on a weekly basis; crews usually find their own provisions; short notice of termination, on either side, is fairly general.

charter party (租船契约)—The document which a Shipowner leases his or her ship to some person or persons, or by which he agrees to carry goods or perform other services. It states the conditions, terms and exceptions that are to prevail in the contract.

DHD (速遣费是滞期费的一半)—despatch half demurrage. Some cargo required to be delivered on time. If the cargo is delivered earlier than the deadline, the carrier will be prized. If the cargo is delivered later than the deadline, the carrier will be punished in double as the prize.

MOLOO (货运量上下限由船东定)—More or less in owner's option. Option allowed to a Shipowner to carry up to a certain quantity, normally expressed as a percentage or a number of tons, over or under a quantity specified in a voyage charter. This option may be sought if the Shipowner is not certain what the ship's cargo capacity will be taking into consideration bunkers, stores and fresh water, or if he wants flexibility to adjust the ship's trim.

WWD (晴天工作日)—Weather working day. Day on which work is normally carried out at a port and which counts as laytime unless loading or discharging would have ceased because of bad weather.

WIPON (无论在港与否)—Whether in port or not. Provision in a voyage charter that the ship does not need to be within the port limits for laytime to start to count. She needs only to arrive at the anchorage, if outside the port, and tender notice of readiness, if required, for laytime to start to count in accordance with charter party.

WOG (大约,没有保障)—Without guarantee. This term is often found in telexes or cables containing details of ships offered on time charter and qualifies, for example, the speed of the ship, designating that this figure is given without commitment.

SB (安全泊位)—Safe berth. Term in a charter party which places the responsibility on to cargo interests to order the chartered ship to berth which is physically safe for her while she is there for the purpose of loading or discharging. A charter-party may contain a clause allowing the charterer to load at one safe berth.

SP (安全港)—Safe port. Term in a charter party which places the responsibility on to cargo interests to order the chartered ship to a port which is physically and politically safe for her to reach, remain at and leave, taking into consideration the cargo to be loaded or discharged. A charter party may contain a clause allowing the charterer to call at one safe port.

CQD (港口习惯装卸速度)—Custom quick dispatch. It is used to describe the loading or discharge rate in laydays in ports. For example, a 2-month layday for loading or discharging of 10,000 tons of ore in a port is not the CQD, but a couple of days layday for the same cargo is the CQD. Hence the CQD is in common sense and it has no definite figure.

AA (总是浮起)—Always afloat. Terms in a charter party which stipulates that the charterer must not order the ship to a port or a berth where she would touch the bottom.

SHEX (星期天及节假日除外)—Sundays and holidays excepted. A charter party term which provides that Sundays and public holidays do not count in the calculation of laytime.

COMM (佣金)—Commission. Money paid for the Agent. In general, it is 2.5% of the freight.

IV. Exercises

1. Discuss with your classmates and answer the following questions.

1) What is the difference between the FOB and the CIF?

2) What is the difference between the Cargo Owner and the Shipowner?

3) Who will pay wages for the Shipmaster and crewmembers in common practice?

4) What is the short word difference between AA and COMM? Please describe them in the method of acronym or abbreviation.

5) Who takes charge of cargo work on board? What is the relationship between the Shipmaster and the Chief Officer on cargo issues?

6) The technical term BENDS refers to both ends. What does the end in the BENDS mean?

7) How important is the English language in maritime logistics?

8) Who takes charge of the Stowage Plan on board the ship?

9) List some cargo documents used in the maritime logistics.

10) What is the role of an insurance company?

2. Deep thinking.

1) What is the difference between cargo agency and ship agency?

2) What does it mean when a Mate's Receipt has been drawn out?

3) What is the meaning of Bill of Lading in the rights of cargo?

4) Why is the term force majeure used in the Sea Protest?

5) Nowadays, the SB or the SP is crucial in shipping business, since the war is potential. Please describe the potential meanings when the safety term is used.

6) When we use the CQD, a reasonable loading or discharge speed is borne in mind. Will you explain the loading or discharging speed for oil, containers, bulk cargo, and general cargo?

7) What is your comprehension on relationships among Shipowner, Cargo Owner, Cargo Agency, and Shipmaster?

8) What is the difference between G. A (general average) and P. A (particular average)?

9) In general, the Shipmaster may sign all receipt on behalf of the Shipowner. What does that imply after the signature?

10) Who will be favourable in the use of the DHD? Please comment.

3.Translate the following sentences into English.

1)物流是指为了满足客户的需求,以最低的成本高效率的完成,通过运输、保管、配送等方式,实现原材料、半成品、成品或相关信息进行由商品的产地到商品的消费地的计划、实施和管理的全过程。

2)承运人,即专门经营水上、陆上、航空等客货运输的部门。如轮船、铁路或公路、航空运输公司等;货主,即专门经营进出口商品业务的外贸部门或进出口商。主要是国际运输中的托运人或收货人;运输代理,即接受委托,代办各种运输业务来收取报酬的人。

3)按船公司经营方式的不同,分为班轮运输和租船运输两种方式。班轮通常是指在预先固定的航线上,按照船期表在固定港口之间来往行驶的船舶;租船运输又称为不定期船运输。

4)承运人与托运人的责任划分:a. 风险以船舷为界;b. 责任和费用的划分界限在船上吊杆所能达到的吊钩底下;c. 承运人义务是按合理的期限将货物完整无损地运到指定地点,并交给收货人。托运人义务是按约定的时间、提供约定的货物,支付运费。

5)附加费指除去基本运费之外加收的费用。是船公司根据不同情况,为了抵补运输中额外增加的开支或蒙受一定损失时而收取的费用。附加费名目繁多主要有:超长和超重附加费、选港附加费、运费贬值附加费、燃油附加费、港口拥挤附加费、绕航附加费、转船附加费和直航附加费等。

4. Translate the following sentences into Chinese.

1) Sixty-six cases of gristles were shipped from Singapore to London under Bills of Lading incorporating the Hague Rules. On arrival twenty-one cases were found to have been broken open and robbed of their contents. It was found to be a reasonable inference that the bristles had been stolen at the loading port. The defendants also proved that they had established a system of watchmen, but they failed to satisfy the court that the watching had actually been carried out vigilantly.

2) As an instance we may refer to the use of shifting boards for the carriage of grain in bulk which is compulsory in certain states. The immediate effect of the breach of such regulations by a shipowner may be to prevent his ship from proceeding from the state in question by refusal of clearance certificates, or to subject him to a penalty when the vessel arrives at a port of such a country without having complied with the said regulations.

3) A Swedish ship was chartered by British shippers. Swedish law required shifting boards for the contemplated bulk grain cargo, but the charter party did not refer to Swedish law; it only provided that the Owners should maintain (the ship) in a thoroughly efficient state in hull, machinery, and equipment for and during the service with dunnage mats, shifting boards (as far as on board), etc.; the owners further warranted the vessel in every way fitted to carry bulk and general cargoes. On these words, it was held that the owners had to pay for additional shifting boards which were required under Swedish law.

4) Apart from owners, many other parties may have a stake in the use and operation of ships. One of the most common relationships is that of charterer and the question therefore arises whether charterers have an insurable interest in the ship they charter. In the case of demise charterer it seems clear that the charterer has at least a possessory interest in the ship which would give him the right to insure. Indeed, standard demise charter agreements can require charterers to keep the vessel insured to protect the interests of both owners and charterers.

5) In a voyage policy a ship is insured for a voyage from one place to another, and the underwriter has to pay for losses happening on the voyage. The Act defines voyage policies as

contracts which insure the subject matter "at and from" or "from one place to another". For voyage policies on ships the time at which the policy attaches depends on which form of wording is used. Voyage policies on cargo on the other hand normally attach, in accordance with the transit clause, when the goods leave the warehouse.

Chapter Four
Culture on Ship Management and Crew Management

第四章
船舶管理和船员管理文化

本章学习目的及本章内容提要

　　本章主要学习船舶管理和船员管理中形成的管理文化；了解船舶种类和不同种类船舶的管理特征，了解船队的规模和船队的管理模式；了解船员的生活与工作方式，以及如何关爱船员；理解中国特色现代企业制度下"党、政、工、团"在船员管理中发挥的巨大作用。

Lesson 10 Familiarization of Types of Ships
第 10 课 熟悉船舶种类

We may use words like ship, boat, craft, ferry, canoe, or skimmer to say a ship. That is the denotative definition rather than the connotative definition. It is not the definition based on the function. "Ship" is the floating unit in terms of margin buoyancy or Archimedes law. The ancient Greek Philosopher Archimedes (287 BCE-212 BCE) found the fact while he was in his bathtub. He described the rule "the buoyancy equals to the weight of the displaced water". Therefore, if the buoyancy of a ship is continuously smaller than the ship's weight, the ship is continually sinking and she will then become a wreck. If the buoyancy equals to ship's weight, the ship keeps floating on the water. If the buoyancy is bigger than the ship's weight, the ship will be rising.

I. Types of Ships on Different Purposes

There are different types of ships in response to the classification methods. For example, the ships are classified in accordance with Charter Parties, including Handysize, Handymax, Suezmax, Panamax, Capesize, and Malaccamax. On the basis of planned routes, the ships are divided into liners and tramps. The liner travels on a prearranged fixed schedule. Containers and cruisers can be arranged in liners easily. The tramp is not in a prearranged fixed schedule.

In general, bulk carriers, general cargo ships, and oil carriers are arranged in tramps easily. In response to the building materials, ships can be classified into steel ships, wood ships, cement ships, and glass reinforced plastic (GRP) ships. On the basis of the numbers of hull in one ship, ships are classified into single hull ship, catamaran, and trimaran. On the basis of the number of decks, vessels are separated into boats (lifeboat, fishing boat, fire-fighting boat) and ships, since a boat has a single deck or it does not have a deck but a ship has several decks. Turning to the purposes, ships are divided into military ships, civilian ships, and specialized ships. In accordance with techniques, the ships are classified into unmanned or unattended machinery space (UMS) ships, smart ships or maritime autonomous surface ships (MASS).

II. Military Ships

Military ships are ships used for military operations. Ships of war are terms in order to avoid the use of warships. In broad concept, war ships are terms for military ships. In a narrow concept, warships are ships used for battle. The group of ships for a particular military mission is called an armada whereas the group of merchant ships is called a fleet (very large scale) or group of ships (small scale).

1. Aircraft Carrier

Aircraft carriers are large vessels to carry aircraft. There are two types of aircraft carriers, namely light aircraft carriers and large aircraft carriers. The displacement varies from 10,000 to 75,000 tons, with carriage of around 120 aircraft. In general, the aircraft carrier will be the flagship in the aircraft armada.

2. Cruiser

Cruisers are large military ships and the displacement is more than 8,000 tons. They are powerful and navigate over long distances. This is why they can travel to distant areas. Chinese cruisers help patrol Somali waters and withdraw Chinese citizens from the warring regions.

3. Destroyer

In general, destroyers are smaller than cruisers. The displacement is less than 8,000 tons. Destroyers are main ships in battle, since the prices of the destroyers are cheaper than most large ships.

4. Frigate

Frigate is also called corvette, or escort vessel. Frigates are military vessels to escort large military vessels. They are also used for fighting. In general, they are the mainstream fighters in most countries. The main task is to undertake tasks such as anti-submarine, escort, patrol, surveillance, reconnaissance, and landing support operations for the naval fleet.

5. Supply Ship

The supply ships are vessels used for provisions replenishments in military use. The ocean-going comprehensive supply ship is a necessary support force for the sea formation to conduct ocean navigation and combat without relying on overseas ports.

6. Landing Ship

Landing ships are used to transport landing troops and weapons and equipment. There are two types of large and medium-sized landing ships, with a displacement of 2,000−8,000 tons and a range of over 3,000 nautical miles. The ship can carry 1,020 tanks and hundreds of landing soldiers. A medium-sized landing ship with a maximum displacement of 600 tons and a range of 1,000 nautical miles, capable of carrying a number of tanks and hundreds of landing soldiers. The landing regulations mostly use diesel engines as the power unit, with the deadweight of 12 tons and the maximum speed of 63 knots.

7. Amphibious Assault Ship

The amphibious assault ship is also called mistral, LHA, IHD, IPH, etc. They are able to carry aircraft, transport tanks, landing forces and other land forces, so its internal design is different from aircraft carriers and many spaces are used to load landing forces. Amphibious assault ships are a kind of warship used to provide air and surface support behind the battle line when fighting in the enemy's coastal areas. It can provide takeoff and landing of shipborne aircraft, ranking second only to aircraft carriers in the Navy.

8. Minesweeper

The minesweeper is a naval surface combatant, which is specially used to clean mines in the sea to protect the safety of navigation channels. The minesweeper generally belongs to second-line combat ships, and the armed forces on board are mainly self-defense. The operation mode of a minesweeper is to navigate back and forth in the sea area suspected of having mines, using the cleaning equipment on board to clear and detonate the mines. The biggest difference in the operational style between minesweepers and minehunters is that minesweepers do not firstly detect the location of individual mines. Therefore, the route and coverage of minesweepers during the clearance process are important to ensure that the cleared waters are not dangerous.

Minesweepers include fleet minesweepers, base minesweepers, harbour minesweepers, and minesweeper carriers. Mainly responsible for opening up navigation channels, clearing mines before landing operations, as well as patrolling, guarding, and escorting tasks.

III. Vessels for Specialised Purposes

There are many special-purpose ships used for engineering or other purposes. Hospital ships are moveable hospitals. Meteorological ships are ships used for weather surveys. Garbage vessels are used to receive garbage at sea. The semi-submersible heavy-load vessel is a vessel used for carrying very large parts. It semi-submerges first. When the large part or wreck is "floating" onto the deck, the ship emerges again. The SAR vessel is a ship used for searching and rescuing and a salvage vessel used for picking up wrecks. The seaplane, the wing-in-ground (WIG), or the hovercraft is amphibious, since it can fly in the air and sail onto water. Tugs are used for towing operations. An icebreaker is a ship used for ice breaking in the icy water. On behalf of the competent authority, the patrol ship is used for surveillance and monitoring in the defined waters. The pilot boat or pilot launch is a ship used for Pilot transfer. The fire float is a ship used for fire-fighting for a large ship if required.

The traffic boat or communication boat is a small boat used for transferring crewmembers from a ship at the anchorage to the shore-side and vice versa. A fishing ship or fishing boat is a vessel used for fishing. A pontoon can also be treated as a float used for storage or other purposes. A floating dry dock (FDD) is a facility used for bottom repair for a large ship in water. It is the extended repair dock in the water. A bunkering ship or bunkering barge is a vessel used for bunkering operation and a skimmer is a ship used for oil cleaning in polluted waters. The bridge will be arranged at the forward for the oil skimmer, the SAR vessel, and the bunker barge in order to make it convenient for the operations. Dredgers are important in clearing fairways in the harbour near the estuary. A survey vessel is a type of ship used for scientific research.

The pile-driving vessel is a ship used for berth building or bridge building, etc. The vessel in servicing is a category to show the engineering operation in the harbour basin or at the fairway. For example, the buoy tender is a type of ship used for maintaining navigation marks. A cable layer is a vessel used for laying cables underwater. The sailing boat, or the entertainment yacht or the recreation yacht is a ship used for entertainment. An obstruction remover is a ship to remove derelicts to keep the fairway safe and clear. A training ship is used for cadet training. A barge or a light aside ship (LASH) is a ship to transfer the cargo from the ship at the anchorage to the berth and vice versa. It may also be used to transfer the cargo from one ship to another ship at the anchorage.

A drilling platform, defined as a mobile offshore drilling unit or short as MODU, is a unit used for drilling out crude oil. A castle carrier is a ship used for carrying castles, such as cows, horses, donkeys, etc. A medical assistance vessel is used for humanitarian assistance. It offers the shipboard hospital for poverties. A restaurant vessel is a mobile restaurant at sea and it offers meals service for passengers.

Ⅳ. Merchant Ships

Merchant ships are civilian ships used for transportation in order to make benefits. There are three kinds of merchant ships, namely ships for carrying cargo, and ships for carrying passengers, ships for carrying passengers and cargo. In American English, merchant ships may be expressed in merchant naval ships. Involving cargo ships, there are solid cargo ships, liquid or liquefied gas ships. Solid cargo ships include general cargo ships, bulk carriers, container ships, etc.

General cargo ships are used to carry different types of cargo, such as cargos in boxes, crates, barrels, drums, bags, sacks, and kraft paper. The OBO, short for oil-bulk-ore ship, is a combination ship used for carrying solid cargo or liquid cargo in bulk. A wood chip ship is a vessel used for carrying pieces of wood, as wood chips are used for paper making. Bulk carriers are vessels used for carrying solid cargo in bulk. The cargo in bulk may include grains, sand, ore, etc. The bulk carrier also includes handy bulk carrier, very large bulk carrier (VLBC), and ultra large bulk carrier (ULBC). The container ship is also a type of solid cargo ship, as the solid cargo is containerized. In this category, the reefer container ship is a container ship with refrigerating system. The feeder container ship is a small container ship used for transferring containers to and fro the large container ships. Hence the feeder container ship with a gantry is normally used. For solid cargo ships, ro/ro ships are widely used. The term ro/ro stands for roll-on/roll-off. In general, there are no gangways' or other means for embarkation and disembarkation of passengers and cargoes, but there are bow ramps, stern ramps, and side ramps instead. A pure car carrier (PCC) is a ro/ro ship used for carrying vehicles and the vehicles can be driven into or out of the ship without using cranes.

Liquid cargo ships are merchant ships used for carrying liquid cargo in bulk. The name for liquid cargo stowage is called tanks whereas the name for solid cargo stowage is called hatches or holds. The liquefied cargo ships include three types, i. e. chemical ships, oil tankers, and liquefied cargo ships. A chemical ship is a ship used for carrying chemicals, such as alcohol, methanol, etc. In common practice, the chemical cargo is liquefied and dangerous. Oil tankers include two types, namely product oil and crude oil. The product oil is refined from crude oil. The product oil includes jet oil, gas oil, diesel oil, kerosene, lubricating oil, fuel oil, paint, and bitumen. In general, the product oil tanker is smaller than the crude oil carrier. The crude oil tanker includes the small crude oil carrier, the very large crude carrier (VLCC) and the ultra large crude carrier (ULCC). The liquefied gas carrier may include liquefied petroleum gas (LPG) carrier and liquefied natural gas (LNG) carrier. On the basis of the sizes of the liquefied gas ships, there are ordinary liquefied gas carrier, very large gas carrier (VLGC), and ultra large gas carrier (ULGC).

Passenger Ships: Passenger ships are used to carry passengers and some are used to carry cargoes. Any ship, which carries more than 12 passengers, is deemed as a passenger ship as per the SOLAS convention. A river ferry is used to transfer passengers or cargo to go a cross the river and some river ferries are used for touring. A ro-ro passenger ship is used to transfer passengers and vehicles. A cruise ship is a large passenger ship used for entertainment and travelling. A cruise ship may carry thousands of passengers. It looks like a large community at sea.

V. Related Culture Words and Technical Terms

armada (n.) (舰队)—It refers to the fleet of military ships. The famous one was the Spanish Armada in the 16th century.

fleet (n.) (船队)—It refers to the group of merchant ships. The fleet is built with many ships. For example, COSCO SHIPPING fleet is composed of hundreds of ships owned by the Company.

group of ships (小型船队)—It implies a ship team which belongs to a company. There is no special word used for the description of a small-scaled fleet in English. In general, group of ships is a term used to describe the ship team for small shipping company.

individual ship(单船船队)—It means a particular ship in a shipping company which owns one ship. In other words it is a group of ships including one ship. It does not refer to a particular ship, but it is a type of ship running in a company. If a ship collides with the facility of a port and causes damages, the port authority may claim compensation. If the compensation is not settled down, the sister ship may be punished as soon as the sister ship visits the port.

flag ship (旗舰)—Warship carrying an admiral in command of a squadron or fleet.

VI. Exercises

1. Discuss with your classmates and answer the following questions.

1) What do the LPG and the LNG stand for?

2）What do the VLBC and the ULBC stand for?

3）What do the VLCC and the ULCC stand for?

4）What is the difference between the SAR vessel and the salvage vessel?

5）There are two types of tugs in common use. What are they?

6）What does the term OBO stand for?

7）Explain the word difference between armada and fleet.

8）What do the acronyms TEU and FEU stand for?

9）What does bulk cargo mean?

10）What does reefer container stand for?

2. Deep thinking.

1）Explain the word "general" in different meanings.

2）Why do Europeans use pilot launch instead of pilot boat?

3）Explain the word structure of the icebreaker. Give more examples of the similar word structure.

4）Why is the term fire float used? What if we call it fire boat?

5）In Chinese, the terms "客滚船" and "客滚码头" are used. What does "客滚" mean? How will you use correct short words in order to avoid ambiguity?

6）Do you think the making of Whale Hunter should be forbidden?

7）What type of metaphor is used in the term ro/ro? Please give a comment.

8）Explain the word differences between cape size and capsize.

9）How to make a difference between the word ship and the word vessel?

10）List the types of ships used for entertainment. Explain the similarities between those vessels.

3. Translate the following sentences into English.

1）从船舶管理者的观点来说,船队分大船队、中小船队、单船船队。其中单船船队在 20 世纪非常普遍,主要是未来规避姊妹船出现与其他方出现纠纷后,连累本船。

2）班轮与不定班轮从船舶种类来看是有一定的区别的,通常集装箱船、邮轮都是班轮,而杂货船、散货船、油船通常是不定班轮。班轮和不定班轮对于船舶管理来说面临着不同的风险与挑战。

3）中国的经济崛起从航运角度来说,也影响着世界,有一种超大散货船就被称为 "Chinamax,是运输从大洋洲或南美洲到中国的超大散货船",这充分说明,世界航运需要中国。

4）《国际海上人命安全公约》规定,载客 12 人以上的船舶即被视为客船,因此有些货船也提供旅客服务,允许个别旅客上船体验,但是无论如何旅客人数必须控制在 12 人以下。

5）船舶种类的分法有很多,比如从建筑材料来看,分为钢板船、水泥船、玻璃钢船,从航线来分,还分为远洋船、近海船、港内作业船、内河船。

4. Translate the following sentences into Chinese.

1）Ro/ro vessels are designed for wheeled cargo, usually in the form of trailers. The cargo can be rapidly loaded and unloaded via ramps or bow doors. Sometimes smaller vehicles are handled via side ports. The cargo-carrying section of the ship is a large, open deck with a loading ramp usually at the after end. Internal ramps lead from the loading deck to the other's tween deck spaces. The cargo may be driven aboard under its own power or loaded by straddle carriers or fork lift trucks. One or more hatches may be provided for containers or general cargo, served by deck cranes. When cargo, with or without wheels, is loaded and discharged by cranes the term lift-on lift-off (Lo-Lo) is used.

2) Bulk cargo is the unpacked cargo of one commodity. Dry bulk cargo is also called bulk carrier normally. Dry bulk cargo such as, grain, ore, fertilizer, etc. are carried in specially designed vessels with hold that have been divided into compartments by longitudinal and transverse separation, so that the ship's stability will not affected by a full cargo. Dry bulk cargo is loaded and discharged by cranes with grabs or suction pipes. Pouring the cargo through a shooter or via a conveyor belt does the loading. Bulk carriers have large upper and lower ballast tanks to give the empty vessel enough draught and better behavior whilst in transit.

3) Refrigerated-cargo vessels are ships that carry perishable cargoes, such as meat or fruit, having a carrying capacity of 8,000-12,000 tons. These cargoes require cooling and must be stored in spaces that have precise temperature and humidity controls during the voyage. Reefers are equipped to carry not only frozen stuff but also goods which first have to be refrigerated to a specific temperature for transportation.

4) Hydrofoil craft makes use of hydrodynamic lift generated by hydrofoils attached to the bottom of the craft. When the craft moves through the water, a lift force is generated to counteract the craft's weight, the hull is raised clear of the water, and the resistance is reduced. High speeds are possible without using unduly large amounts of power. Once the hull is clear of the water, and therefore not contributing buoyancy, the lift required of the foils is effectively constant. As speed increases, either the submerged area of foil will reduce, or their angle of incidence must be reduced.

5) Cargo ships that carry both general cargo, bulk cargo and containerized cargo are called multi-purpose vessels. These vessels are equipped with a variety of cargo handling gears to load and discharge the different types of cargo. These ships use hatch covers as bulkheads as well as tween decks in the hold. These hatch covers can be placed at varying heights and positions. Usually, the head ledges and hatch coamings are of the same dimensions as the holds, which makes loading and discharging easier. The holds are sealed with hatches using a variety of systems. Cargoes like wood or containers can be carried on the top of the hatches. Often the bulwark is heightened to support the containers.

Lesson 11   Ship Manning, Working and Living Styles
第 11 课   船上配员、工作和生活方式

The term manning means to man personnel on board a ship or on board ships. In general, manning is a technical term rather than an HR term.

There are different words used to describe working staff on board, such as crew, crewmember, sailor, seafarer, mariner, seaman, salty, navigator, new joiner, fresher, etc. Although each word has peculiar meanings, they share the same meaning of the key worker in water transport. On board ships, manning persons are divided into three levels, namely management level, operation level, and support level. The management level is called the top 4, including the Shipmaster, the Chief Engineer, the Chief Officer, and the Second Engineer. The operational level is in the middle and it includes the Second Officer, the Third Engineer, the ETO, the Third Officer, and the Fourth Engineer. The support level is the lowest level and all other crewmembers are in this group. The Shipmaster and all the crewmembers will be introduced hereinafter.

I . Manning on Board

1. Shipmaster

A Shipmaster may be called the Captain, the Master, the Skipper (for small vessels or boats), Lifeboatman (the leader on board a lifeboat), the Old Man (indirect calling among Deck Officers), and the like. A Shipmaster is the representative of the Shipowner and he or she is the top leader on board a ship. The Shipmaster is never deemed as one of crewmembers on board a ship, but he or she is the shipping company employee to work on board the ship. He or she owns overriding authority in case of emergency. He or she has the rights to dismiss any crewmember on board the ship as per good safety management system and common practices. He or she is always responsible for the ship. Although familiarizing the navigation knowledge, he or she is not the leader of the deck department, but he or she is the leader of the entire ship. For most duties, he or she monitors the deck department staff and he or she monitors the engine department staff via the status of the mission completion.

He or she looks like a node or a bridge among the Shipowner, Cargo Owners, Charterers, Consignors, Consignees, Port State Control Officers (PSCOs), Flag State Control Officers (FSCOs), Immigration Officers, Customs and Quarantine Officers, Cargo Surveyors, Ship Surveyors, Superintendents, Chief Policemen, Port Captain, and other personnel from different parties.

2. Manning in the Deck Department

Chief Officer

In general, the Shipmaster calls him the Chief Mate or the Mate, the First Mate. In some cases, the Chief Officer is called the First Officer. The Chief Officer is the first leader of the deck department and he or she is the second leader of the ship. If the Shipmaster is not on board (such as shore tours, ill, or dead), the Chief Officer will be the temporary Shipmaster on board until the Shipmaster returns or a new Shipmaster takes over. Similarly, he or she will be taken over by the Shipmaster if he or she is not on board.

He or she is responsible for cargo operation (such as stowage plan, stability calculation, loading, discharging or unloading, cargo care, ventilation, cooling, and drying) on board. He or she is the leader on spot or on scene during distress or emergency (such as fire, explosion, flooding or making water, grounding or stranding, pollution, cargo damage, armed attack, piracy, sinking or foundering, capsizing, collision, allision, loss or damage, pilfering, contact, abandoning ship, etc.).

He or she also keeps watch duty (navigation watch) when at sea or in harbour, or in the anchorage, or mooring a buoy, or in single berthing mooring (SBM) or single point mooring (SPM). The watch periods are 0400–0800 and 1600–2000. He or she is responsible for control and communicate operations at the forecastle deck during mooring, unmooring, shifting, anchoring, heaving up anchor, etc.

For particular vessels such as oil tankers, the Chief Officer takes no navigation watch duties. Therefore the vessels will be fitted with two Second Officers or two Third Officers. One of the Second Officers or the Third Officers will watch at 0400–0800 and 1600–2000.

Second Officer

The Second Officer is also called the Second Mate and the Shipmaster and the Chief Officer may call him the Second. He or she is the second leader of the deck department.

He or she keeps watch duty (navigation watch, gangway watch, cargo watch, security watch) when at sea or in harbour, or in the anchorage, or mooring a buoy, or in single berth mooring or in single point mooring during 0000–0400 and 1200–1600 every day.

He or she will prepare to take over the Third Officer's duty if the Third Officer is not on board. He or she is responsible for chart work and passage plan and he or she is responsible for navigation equipment and navaids (navigational aids). He or she is responsible for keeping nautical publications (such as IMO conventions, *Admiralty publications*, *Admiralty Sailing Directions*, *Admiralty Lists of Lights and Fog Signals*, *Admiralty Tide Tables*, *Admiralty Lists of Radio Signals*, *International Code of Signals*, *Guide to Port Entry*, *Medical Guide for the Shipmaster*). He or she is responsible for mooring or unmooring, anchoring operation at the stern or poop deck during mooring, unmooring, shifting, anchoring dropping or heaving, etc.

Third Officer

The Third Officer is also called the Third Mate and the Shipmaster, the Chief Officer, the Second Officer call him or her the Third. The Third Officer keeps watch duty (navigation watch, gangway watch, cargo watch, security watch) during 0800 – 1200 and 2000 – 2400. He or she is responsible for fire-fighting appliances (FFAs) and life-saving appliances (LSAs). He or she is responsible for preparation of navigation on the bridge. He or she takes over the Second Officer's duties if the Second Officer is not on board. He or she is responsible for mooring or unmooring, anchoring operation on the bridge during mooring, unmooring, shifting, anchoring dropping or heaving, etc. He or she is responsible for picking up the Pilot during mooring, unmooring, shifting, anchor dropping or heaving, when the Pilot is ordered.

Radio Officer

Before the implementation of the Global Maritime Distress and Safety System laid down in Chapter 4 of the SOLAS 1988 amendment, a Radio Officer was manned on board. Nowadays, the radio staff with the First Class Radio Electronic Certificate Holder or the Second Class Radio Electronic Certificate shall be manned on board according to the STCW convention. However, the radio personnel are not necessary if two or more general operator's certificate holders are on board ships. The general operator's certificate (GOC) is a part of certificates for Deck Officers. In addition, the restricted operator's certificate (ROC) holder is necessary on board ships exclusively navigating in inland waters.

Ratings in Deck Department

The bosun or boatswain is the working leader of the sailor. He or she is one of the idle persons on board. He or she is the foreman of sailors. Under the order of the Chief Mate, he or she arranges daily maintenance and repair work. He or she is responsible for bosun's store which paints, spare parts, stores, tools are inside. He or she is responsible for arranging sailors' watch duties under the direction of the Chief Officer. He or she is responsible for arranging sailors' maintenance and repair group, under the direction of the Chief Mate. He or she will take over the duties if the cassab or the carpenter is not on board. Likewise, he or she will also be taken over by the cassab or the carpenter if he or she is not on board. He or she is the foreman of the sailors in the deck department. He or she will prepare the pilot ladder or gangway before picking up a Pilot or getting alongside. He or she will be the foreman on the poop deck when mooring, unmooring, shifting, anchoring operation. A cassab is the deputy bosun. This position has been replaced by the carpenter on board most ships. On board cruise ships, cassabs may be manned to take charge of daily repair work on deck. He or she is one of the idle persons on board. Under the direction of the Chief Officer and the bosun, he or she is the leader of the sailor groups in the maintenance and repair on spot. He or she is responsible for bosun's duty work if the bosun is absent, ill, or dead on board. The carpenter is one of the idle persons on board. He or she is responsible for sounding water tanks daily. He or she is responsible for keeping damage control materials. On the forecastle deck, he or she is responsible for operating deck machinery, such as windlass, mooring winch, tension winch, deck crane, mechanism for hatch operation, when mooring, unmooring, anchoring, and shifting. He or she is responsible for repairing furniture. He or she will take over the cassab or even the bosun's duties if the cassab or the bosun is not on board. Likewise, he or she will be taken over by the bosun or the cassab if he or she is not on board. He or she is responsible for the draining system in the accommodation area (living spaces, cargo spaces, superstructure, living quarters). Sailors are divided into able seafarer deck (ASD) or able body (AB), and ordinary seaman (OS). The able body is responsible for maintaining and repairing on deck daily. He or she is responsible for watch duties on conning bridge as the helmsman or the quartermaster. A helmsman or quartermaster means a sailor who works in the wheelhouse to take the helm under the direction of the Shipmaster, the OOW or the Pilot.

3. Catering Department

The catering department or the service department used to be a separate department on board merchant ships. On board cruise ships, the catering department may be divided into galley department, entertaining department, casino, hotel department, touring department, etc. Nowadays, the catering department is attached to the deck department on board merchant ships. In that case, the Shipmaster, the Chief Mate or other Deck Officer may be the Purser-leader of the department. The word purser is derived from the word purse, which means billfold or wallet. The Purser is a person who owns a purse. On board training ships and passenger ships, the Exclusive Purser is the leader of the department. He or she is responsible for the catering department. He or she is responsible for vouchers (invoice), bills and accounts, cash or currency on board. The chief steward will temporarily take over the Purser's duties if the Purser is not on board.

The chief cook or chef is the foreman of cooks. He or she is responsible for galley work on board. He or she is responsible for making menus. Under the direction of purser, he or she is responsible for frozen locker and bonded store. He or she will take over the second cook's duty if the second cook is absent on board. Second cook is the worker in the galley. Under the direction of the Purser (Chief Officer) and the chief cook, the second cook makes meals for all crewmembers. Under the direction of the chief cook, the second cook cleans the galley before and after cooking. Under the direction of the chief cook, the second cook makes cake, bread, and rice for crewmembers. Under the direction of the chief cook, the second cook washes vegetables and chips.

The chief steward is the senior waiter on board. Under the direction of the Shipmaster, the Chief Officer, and the Purser, the chief steward is responsible for cleaning Senior Officers' offices and meeting rooms, saloons, etc. The chief steward serves Pilots, Agents, sea policemen, immigration officers, customs officers, ship surveyors, cargo surveyors, port captains, staffs from the port authority, the chief tallyman, the chief stevedore or the chief longshoreman, the tugman, the linesman, the bargeman, or other guests, kins or relatives of crewmembers from shore-side. The chief steward will be taken over by the boy if the chief steward is absent. Most chief stewards are females on board Russian and East European ships. He or she is responsible for serving Senior Officers' meals if the Senior Officers' messrooms are different from the ratings' messrooms. He or she is responsible for serving meals for all crewmembers if the boy is absent. The chief steward is responsible for cleaning Senior Officers' corridors, laundries, Shipmaster's office and Chief Engineer's office, etc.

The boy or steward is a junior waiter on board ships. Sometimes, the chief steward is short as steward and steward is short for boy. Nowadays, there is only one waiter called steward on board common merchant ships. The boy's responsibilities are as follows: Under the direction of the Shipmaster, the Chief Mate, and the Purser, the boy is responsible for cleaning messrooms, serving meals for all crewmembers and washing dishes after meals. The boy is responsible for cleaning ratings' corridors, laundries, etc. The boy will take over the chief steward's duties if the chief steward is absent and vice versa. The Surgeon or the Medical Officer is a person who serves medical work on board. The Chief Mate or the Second Mate serves the Medical Officer if the Surgeon is not manned on board. The Surgeon is a professional doctor with the doctor's license. The Surgeon is responsible for maintaining the hospital and medicines. The Surgeon is responsible for controlled medicine, but the Medical Officer has no right to use controlled medicine. Only under the authorization of the Shipmaster, the controlled medicine is ready for use if the Surgeon is not manned on board. The Surgeon will be the leader of the first aid team and he manages first aid kit or first aid box, stretcher or litter, CPR in an emergency or drills.

4. Engine Department

The engine department, as the name suggests, is the department to guarantee the smooth running of the engines and machines.

Chief Engineer

The Shipmaster calls the Chief Engineer the Chief. The Chief Engineer is always responsible for all engines and machinery. He or she is the top leader (management, executive) and technical consultant of the engine department. He or she is under the direction of the Shipmaster. He or she is responsible for arranging work for the engine staff. He or she will take over the duties of the Second Engineer if the Second Engineer is not on board. Likewise, the Second Engineer will take over the Chief Engineer's duties if the Chief Engineer is not present.

Second Engineer

The Second Engineer is also called the first assistant Chief Engineer or the First Engineer in East Asia and the Shipmaster and the Chief Engineer may call him or her the Second. The Second Engineer is the executive leader of the engine department. He or she is responsible to maintain the main propulsion plant main engine or horse engine including main engine, shafting system, thrust bearing, tail bearing, driving shaft, intermediate shaft, tail shaft, shaft tunnel, propeller and steering gear. On board some ships, the Second Engineer may take charge of refrigerating system and air-conditioning system. He or she keeps the watch duties during 0400 – 0800, and 1600—2000 daily. He or she is responsible for arranging watch duties (Executive Officer) for all motormen. He or she will take over the Chief Engineer's duties if the Chief Engineer is not on board.

Third Engineer

The Third Engineer is also called the second assistant Chief Engineer or the Second Engineer in East Asia. His or her responsibilities are as follows: Under the direction of the Chief Engineer and Second Engineer, he or she is responsible for prime movers of generators (auxiliary engine or donkey engine). The generators may include main generators, backup generators, shaft generators, and emergency generators. If the ETO is not available on board, the Third Engineer is also responsible for the power plant, including generators, switchboards, and electric loads. The Third Engineer is also responsible for other power systems, such as air bottles for all purposes, oil purifiers, and boilers. He or she keeps watch duties during 0000 – 0400 and 1200 – 1600 hours daily. The Third Engineer takes over the Fourth Engineer's duties if the Fourth Engineer is not on board.

Fourth Engineer

The Fourth Engineer is called the third assistant Chief Engineer or the Third Engineer in East Asia. The leaders may call him or her the Fourth. The main responsibilities are as follows: Under the direction of the Chief Engineer and Second Engineer, he or she is responsible for auxiliary machinery, such as anti-pollution equipment (including oily water separator with 15 ppm alarm, sewage treatment plant, flue gas treatment plant, scrubber, and incinerator), deck machinery (including windlass, mooring winch, tension winch, deck crane, mechanism for opening and closing hatches, capstan, cargo winch), boilers, pumps. He or she keeps watch duties during 0800 – 1200 and 2000 – 2400 hours local time daily. He or she will temporarily take over the Third Engineer's duties if the Third Engineer is not on board. Likewise, he or she will be temporarily taken over by the Third Engineer if the Third Engineer is not on board.

Electro Technical Officer

The electro Technical Officer (ETO) is a new position as per STCW Manila. The word electro includes electric and electronic. The ETO is in the operation level. The position is on the same level as the Second Officer and the Third Engineer. In the old system, the ETO was called electrical engineer or electrical officer. He or she is one of the idle persons on board. The responsibilities are as follows: He or she is responsible for all electrical parts on board. He or she is responsible for the electrical installations, such as generators electrical motors, switchboards, electrical loads, electrical cables, electrical drive system, etc. He or she is responsible for maintaining all domestic electrical machines on board. He or she is responsible for electrical parts of navigation equipment, navaids, and communication equipment on the bridge. He or she is responsible for all electrical parts of all engines and machines in the engine room. He or she is responsible for all electrical parts of deck machinery. His or her duties are replaced by the Third Engineer if the ETO is not available on board.

If he or she is temporarily absent, he or she will be replaced by the Third Engineer or even the Chief Engineer.

Ratings in the Engine Department

In the ratings group, there are a head oiler, a storeman, a fitter, wipers, motormen, pumpmen, an electrician, etc. The head oiler is also called foreman, or No. 1 oiler, or No. 1 motorman. He or she is an idle person on board. Under the direction of the Chief Engineer as well as the Second Engineer, the head oiler is responsible for arranging duty watches and repair work. Under the direction of the Chief Engineer and the Second Engineer, the head oiler is responsible for overtime charge calculation. The head oiler is the leader of all workers in the engine department.

The storeman or storekeeper used to be an important position on board. It is deemed as deputy foreman in some cases. He or she is an idle person on board. Under the direction of the Chief Engineer, the Second Engineer and the head oiler, he or she keeps stores, spare parts, tools and workshops. Under the direction of those leaders, he or she calculates the stores, spare parts, and tools weekly, monthly, and yearly as per the company's rules. He or she will take over the head oiler's duties if the head oiler is not on board. Likewise, he or she will be taken over by the head oiler if he or she is not on board.

The electrician or the electro technical rating (ETR), as the name recommends, is a crewmember for maintaining electricity under the direction of the Chief Engineer or the Second Engineer. A pumpman is a person to maintain and repair pumps. A fitter is a person for welding work and a wiper is the cleaner in the engine department. The donkeyman has nothing to do with donkey. The word donkey refers to auxiliary in the word donkeyman, so a donkeyman is a person to do maintenance and repair work for auxiliary engines or auxiliary machinery. The oiler is also called as the motorman, the greaser instead. Under the direction of the Chief Engineer, the Second Engineer, and the head oiler, they maintain and repair the engines and machinery on board. They will attend the duty watches as per the instructions from their leaders. They will attend the emergency repairs while the critical engines or machines are in failure.

II. Living and Working Styles

In general, there are two types of working styles on board ships, namely idlers and watchkeepers. The Shipmaster, the Chief Engineer, the ETO, the purser, the bosun, the cassab, the steward, the head oiler, the carpenter, the storeman, and the ETR are the idlers whereas other crewmembers are watchkeepers. Watchkeepers shall keep a watch twice every 24 hours. Good rest shall be kept in order to get energy before the next watch. All crewmembers are not permitted to drink alcohol within 6 hours of the next watch start. The Third Officer or the Shipmaster may relieve the watch at the breakfast time and the supper time, so the Chief Officer can use the breakfast and supper on time. The Fourth Engineer or the Chief Engineer may also take the watch temporarily on the breakfast time and supper time to let the Second Engineer use the meals in good time. In general, the breakfast is arranged on 0700 hours, and the lunch is arranged on 1200 hours, and the supper is arranged on 1700 hours. If there is a night watch, a snack will be arranged at night.

Ⅲ. Entertainment

After work, crewmembers may choose to read books, do physical fitness, watch videos, do jogging on the running machine, swim in the tiny swimming pool, chat with other persons, or surf on the Internet. Nutritional foods are arranged by the catering department.

Ⅳ. Crew Management

Crewmembers are significant human resources. In·common practice, the crewmembers are organized in crew management companies. While the crewmembers wish to work on board, the employment contract will be signed by the crew, the Shipowner, and the Agent from the crew management company.

The crew management company is responsible for offering competent crewmembers to shipowners who are deemed as the customers of the crew management company. The crew management company is the agent for the crewmembers organized in the company. The crew management company is responsible for:

—recruitment of qualified crewmembers or potential crewmembers for nurturing;

—caring for all crewmembers and their families;

—communicating with the shipping companies on the promotions of the crewmembers;

—arranging claims to the shipping company if accidents (illness, death, injury cases) incurred;

—arranging travel if repatriations are decided;

—arranging the examinations on CoCs;

—arranging the pensions if part of deposits will be given to the social assurance system;

—settling some problems occurred on board and communicating with the shipping company;

—arranging employment interviews in cooperation with the crew manning department of the shipping company;

—organizing short-term training for crewmembers in order to keep safety at sea in the future work.

Ⅴ. Related Culture Words and Technical Terms

recreation room (娱乐室)—In accordance with MLC 06, the ship shall be fitted with a recreation room for all crewmembers. They may use the recreation room for game playing, jogging in the running machine, and video watching.

hours local time（当地时间）—In common practice, the local time will be used in the ship operation. The time will be expressed in four digits. For instance, ten o'clock will be expressed in 1000 hours local time.

GMT（格林尼治平时）and **UTC**（协调世界时）—GMT stands for Greenwich Mean Time. It is a time in zero time zone. It used to be a reference time in the world. UTC（Universal Time Coordinated）, recommended by BIH（世界时间协会）, had replaced GMT since 1981.

Harbour Master or **Port Captain**（港长）—Official having superintendence over a harbour; and who is responsible for harbour regulations which should be complied with.

alcohol beware（谨防酗酒）—Crewmembers are not fouled with chore such as preparing meals. In that case crewmembers get more free time. In order to cheer themselves, some crewmembers committed alcohol. That impacts the safety of life and the ship. Shipping company has strict rules on alcohol.

seasickness（*n.*）（晕船）—As the name suggests, persons are sick in waves. One of the least pleasant aspects on board is the possibility of seasickness. An individual's susceptibility to seasickness is highly variable. Most people feel some level of illness or discomfort when they first go to sea.

homesickness（*n.*）（想家）—While the ship is far away from the land, crewmembers may miss families and relatives. Albeit those senses do not impact on the safety of the ship, those influence the qualities of lives at sea.

drug problem（药品和毒品问题）—Crewmembers have chances to get drugs. Dolantin, codeine, and morphine used for broken bone cases and cancers may get addicted. Herein, opium, and marijuana are drugs. All shipping companies have set up rules to beware of the abuse of drugs.

HR（人力资源）—It stands for human resources. It is widely used in crew management.

crew and **seafarer**（船员）—Crew and seafarer are technical terms which refer to seafarers works on board. Crew is commonly used in the management system, since a team may be imagined while talking about crew. However, the term seafarer is commonly used in recent years. It implies qualified seaman on board ships. A typical example is the word seafarer used in the STCW convention. The seafarer also means that the seaman works on an ocean-going vessel.

pension（*n.*）（养老金）—Money shall be deposited while the seafarer works. After the retire, the seafarer will get the money back as a kind of wages. While the seafarer works, the crew management company will collect the money and pay for the public service.

retention ratio（持有率）—A retention ratio is a figure to show the percentage of crewmembering working in the shipping company. For example, 100 cadets were enrolled in a shipping company and 29 of them still work in the fleet. The retention ratio is 29%.

crew pool（船员行业）—It is a metaphor to say the crew industry. The trade looks like a swimming pool. When they want to work on board, they join in. When they don't want to work on board, they quit. That looks like the functions of the swimming pool.

P&I club（船东互保协会）—It stands for protection and indemnity. A group of shipowners establish an "insurance" company. They establish a fund for the use when ships suffered from damages or their crewmembers were injured.

Ⅵ. Exercises

1. Discuss with your classmates and answer the following questions.

1) What does the top 4 mean?

2) What is the management level defined in the STCW convention?

3) What is the operational level defined in the STCW convention?

4) What is the operational level defined in the STCW convention?

5) What do the term ASD and the term ASE stand for?

6) What do the term AB and the term OS mean?

7) Who will pay the crewmembers, the shipowner or the crew management company?

8) What are terms for the Shipmaster?

9) How many departments are there on board a ship?

10) What kind of difficulties will the seafarers encounter when they work on board?

2. Deep thinking.

1) What is your comprehension of the standard of competence for crewmembers?

2) Do you think the Shipmaster is an integral part of crewmembers? Give us your comments.

3) Why is the pool used in the crew pool? What is the type of metaphor?

4) Explain the values of the maritime universities or colleges based on the retention ratio calculated by the shipowner or the management company.

5) Do you think a cadet should be an Officer or a rating?

6) What is the meaning of idler? Why are they called idlers?

7) Please explain the living and working styles on board. Please give them some recommendations.

8) Why do crewmembers keep local time working and living principles? Please explain the advantages.

9) Explain the relationships between the Shipmaster and the Chief Engineer in your understanding.

10) If a crewmember was injured, how would he or she get the premium?

3. Translate the following sentences into English.

1) 中华人民共和国海事局船员处负责船员管理工作,具体包括组织起草船员管理的相关法律、法规、规章草案和规范性文件,并监督实施,还负责组织船员管理质量体系的建立、运行和管理。

2) 船员管理公司是专门负责将船员派出工作的公司。它们还负责船员上下船的旅行安排,负责船员工伤赔偿、船员升职等相关事宜。

3）船员证书管理也是船员管理公司的工作之一，船员管理公司需要掌握所属公司的船员证书信息，比如换证与考证等都需要及时提醒船员。

4）在我国船员在晋升大副、大管轮、船长、轮机长之前需要到指定的培训机构做强制性的培训，而联系培训机构也是船员管理公司的职责之一。

5）自实施《ISM 规则》以后，船员管理公司和船东必须分离，在签署"船员雇用合同"时，必须有船东、船员、船员管理公司三方，以保障船员的合法权益得到第三方见证。

4. Translate the following sentences into Chinese.

1）Good teamwork is about relationships among team members. It concerns each team member understanding their role and contribution to the group and feeling valued for the part they play in helping the team succeed. When relationships are respectful, valuing and positive, the sky's the limit! Team Dynamics are the unseen forces that operate in a team among different people or groups. Team Dynamics can strongly influence how a team reacts, behaves or performs.

2）The standards of competence that will need to be achieved for each of these functions are defined at up to three levels of responsibility, which are explained in the STCW Code as follows:

The management level means the level of responsibility associated with serving as the Shipmaster, the Chief Mate, the Chief Engineer or the Second Engineer Officer on board of sea-going ships, and ensuring that all the functions within the designated area of responsibility are properly performed. The operational level means the level of responsibility associated with: serving as officer in charge of navigational or engineering watch or as designated duty engineer for periodically unmanned machinery spaces or as radio operator on board a seagoing ship, and maintaining direct control over the watch.

3）Seasickness is a result of a conflict in the inner ear (where the human balance mechanism resides) caused by the erratic motion of the ship through the water. Inside the cabin of a rocking boat, for example, the inner ear detects changes in linear and angular acceleration as the body bobs with the boat. But since the cabin moves with the passenger, the eyes register a relatively stable scene. Agitated by this perceptual incongruity, the brain responds with a cascade of stress-related hormones that can ultimately lead to nausea and vomiting.

4）The Captain ensures that the ship complies with local and international laws and complies also with company and flag state policies. The Captain is ultimately responsible, under the law, for aspects of operation such as the safe navigation of the ship, its cleanliness and seaworthiness, safe handling of all cargo, management of all personnel, inventory of the ship's cash and stores, and maintaining the ship's certificates and documentation.

5）A sea Captain, Master Mariner, ship's Captain, Captain, Master, or Shipmaster, is a high-grade licensed mariner who holds ultimate command and responsibility of a merchant vessel. The Captain is responsible for the safe and efficient operation of the ship including its seaworthiness, safety and security, cargo operations, navigation, crew management, and legal compliance and for the persons and cargo on board.

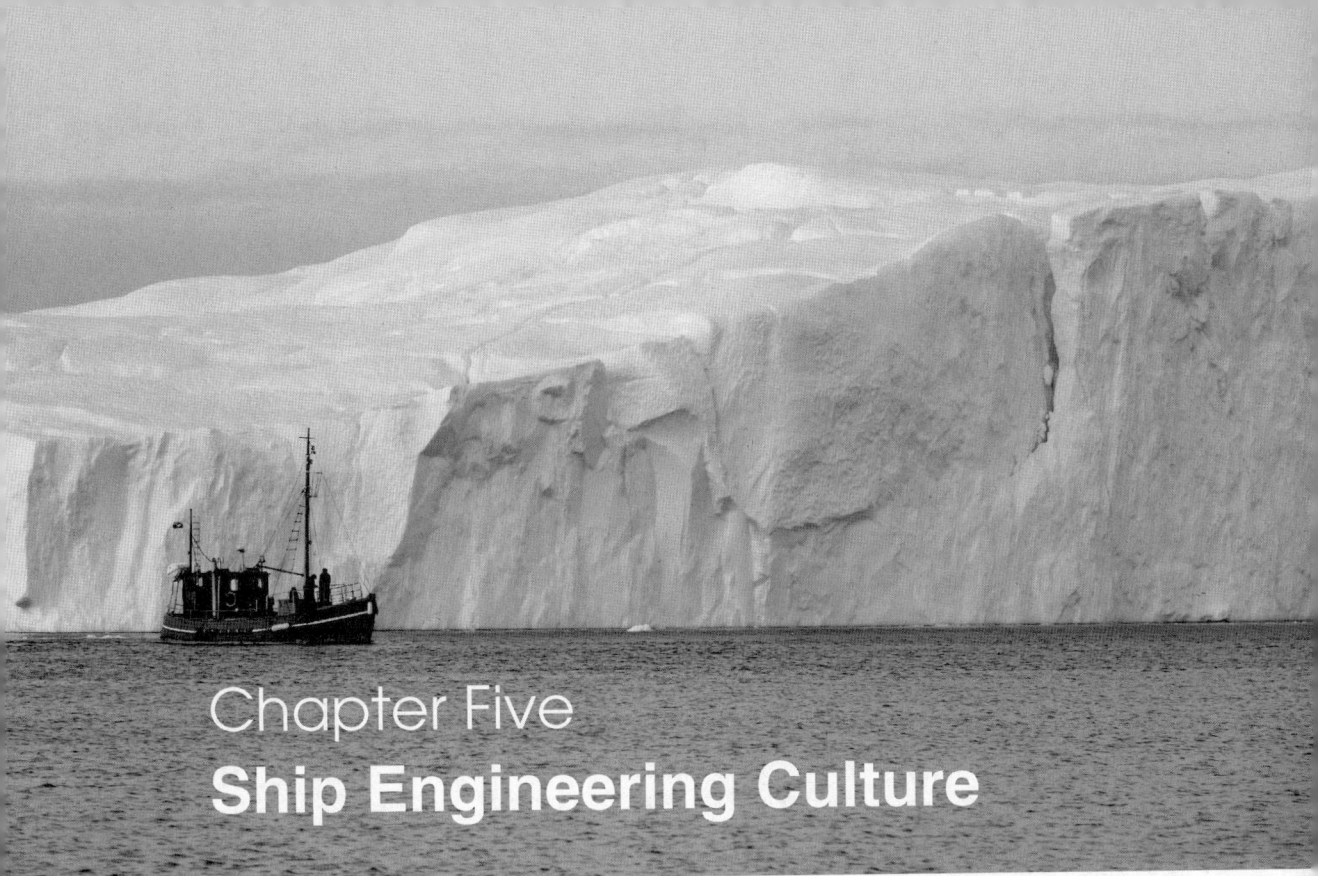

Chapter Five
Ship Engineering Culture

第五章
船舶工程文化

本章学习目的及本章内容提要

　　本章主要学习船舶工程概况和船舶工程文化。了解中国船舶建造历史和中国从古至今船舶工程最灿烂的文化；了解中华人民共和国成立后船舶工程的发展成就和船舶工程主管机关；了解船舶建造的概况、船舶维修的基本情况，了解海洋工程等相关信息，为未来服务航运强国做知识铺垫。

Lesson 12　History of Shipbuilding in China
第 12 课　中国船舶建造史

As early as the Neolithic Age（10000 BCE-4000 BCE）, our ancestors were capable of making canoes and rafts. It was reported that Southeastern Chinese began to build canoes to navigate at sea.

Ⅰ. Early Shipbuilding Records in China

According to the record in the *Book of Changes*（易经）,"刳木为舟，剡木为楫。"（To hollow out a wood trunk as a canoe and to chip a wood as an oar.）was recorded. It lodges Gonggu（共鼓）and Huodi（货狄）, two Ministers of Huangdi（黄帝）, were empowered to make canoes. Huangdi Period was around 2697 BCE. That is to say, the first shipbuilding had already commenced 5,000 years ago. It was almost at the end of the Neolithic Age. Since there was no nail in very ancient time, our ancestors made the canoe with hollowing out（empty）the trunk. To chip the wood to make oars. They realized the floating theory（Archimedes law,阿基米德定律）. They knew how to keep floating on the water.

Ⅱ. Different Types of Chinese Ships in Ancient Times

In the upstream of the Yellow River, sheep skins are also used for the floating unit buildings. They sewed sheep skins and charged air as the floating units. Several sheep float units lashed a raft. This floating unit was used to transit the Yellow River.

In the Qin Dynasty, ships in the Yellow River were called *Bo*（舶）whereas ships in the Yangtze River were called *Bian*（艑）. Ships were divided into different types from the earlier Warring States. *Yuhuang*（余皇）was the ship for royal use in that period. *Shenzhou*（神舟）was a kind of ship for diplomatic use in the Song Dynasty. *Doujian*（斗舰）was a battle used during late Han and entire Tang Dynasty and *Wuyajian*（五牙舰）was a type of ship for military use in the early Sui Dynasty. *Fang*（舫）was a large cruiser and *Yudaniang*（俞大娘）was a kind of large cruiser in the Tang Dynasty. *Louchuan*（楼船）was a large ship used from the early Warring States to the Ming Dynasty. *Mengchong*（艨艟）was the small battle ship in very ancient time and *Haiqiuchuan*（海鳅船）was an inland battle ship in the Song Dynasty. *Mulanzhou*（木兰舟）was the large seagoing ship in the Song Dynasty. *Baochuan*（宝船）was the vessel used by Zheng He fleet. *Xunzuochuan*（巡座船）was the patrol ship in inland waters in the Ming Dynasty. Dragon boat was the ship used for boat competition in

Duanwu festival（dragon festival）, etc. *Zhameng*（蚱蜢）ship looked like a grasshopper, because of narrow shape used in the river. Sampan was the common boat used for quite long time and it is widely used now. *Ge*（舸）was a large vessel sailing in the river or at sea. *Jian*（舰）was the military ship and it was small from very beginning, since the bed berths for crewmembers were in layers. The accommodation space was very narrow. *Ling*（舲）was a river boat in Zhejiang and Jiangsu starting from the early Warring States. Pontoon（浮船）as the bridge was created in the early Warring States. *Ta*（塌）was a large vessel used for quite a long time. *Nanhaichuan*（南海船）, similar but earlier than *Zhenghebaochuan*（郑和宝船）, was used as the oceangoing vessel in the Tang Dynasty.

III. Different Types of Chinese Ships in Different Waters in China

With the development of shipbuilding in China, there are different types of ships in different areas. *Caochuan*（漕船）is a kind of barges used in the Grand Canal to carry official commodities, such as salt, grains, etc. *Changshabanbo*（长沙板驳）, which the bottom is flat, was the common boat used in Xiangjiang River（湘江）. *Danyangchuan*（丹阳船）was a boat transited in Fujian waters and *Dengguanchuan*（邓关船）was a boat sailing in Tuojiang River（沱江）of Sichuan. *Duolongzichuan*（舵笼子船）was a boat sailing in Yicang band of Changjiang（the Yangtze River）. *Piaochuan*（瓢船）was a boat sailing in Shannxi（陕西）band of the Yellow River. *Quechuan*（雀船）was a ship sailing in Minjiang River, Fujian. *Fushaozichuan*（浮梢子船）was a boat sailing in Poyang Lake. *Wujiangzichuan*（乌江子船）was a boat sailing in Xiangjiang River, Hunan. *Bailuchuan*（白鹭船）was a type of ships sailing in Fujian and *Yashaochuan*（鸦艄船）was a boat Xiaogan, Hubei. *Hezichuan*（盒子船）, which the middle part looks like a box, was widely used in Dianchi, Yunnan and *Jiangjichuan*（江鸡船）was a boat sailing in Yalujiang, Liaoning. *Daoyuchuan*（鲂鱼船）was a kind of high speed craft sailing in Jiangsu and Zhejiang in the Song Dynasty. *Huchuan*（唬船）was a boat popularly used in Zhejiang and Fujian in the Ming and Qing Dynasties.

IV. Shipbuilding in Ancient China

Shipbuilding in the Qin Dynasty

During the war to the south state, Qinshihuang（嬴政）sent a large fleet to carry troops and grain. It follows that a large shipbuilding was achieved at that time. The rudder was designed at that period of time.

Shipbuilding in the Han Dynasty

Large superstructured ships were built in the Han Dynasty. The purpose of large ship building is for the war. At that time ships were divided into different types used for battle. Long and slim boats were built to gain the fast speed. Double hulled ships were built to gain heavy strength. In the Three Kingdom period, *Chibi battle*（赤壁战船）is a large war in terms of ships and boats. Paddle ships were built at that time.

Shipbuilding in the Sui, Tang and Song Dynasties

In 640 CE, Suiyangdi（杨广）ordered to build large dragon ships and he wanted to tour Yangzhou in the Grand Canal. The largest one is a floating palace ship. The length is around 60 metres and the height is 15 metres. There are more than 120 cabins on board the ship. The connections in the shipbuilding are Sun and Mao wood structures. Sail boat building was popular in the Tang Dynasty. Famous Poets wrote many poems concerning sailing boat. That is a typical example.

Zhenghe Ships in the Ming Dynasty

Zhenghe ships are unique. The ships are large, square, and high. The forward part is sharp but the stern is flat. The watertight compartments were used in the shipbuilding at that time. Those ships were safe and comfortable while sailing at sea. Zhenghe ships were the largest ships in the world.

V. Related Culture Words and Technical Terms

ship constructed（船舶起建）—It means ships the keels of which are laid or which are at a similar stage of construction.

a similar stage of construction（相似建造阶段）—It means the stage at which construction identifiable with a specific ship begins; and assembly of that ship has commenced comprising at least 50 tonnes or 1% of the estimated mass of all structural material, whichever is less.

natural rules in philosophy（自然规律在哲理中）—To hollow out a tortoise shell, the efficacious divination can be achieved. Without a medium insertion, the effective magnetic force for the pair of magnets will functionate. With a cavited core, a bell or a drum can be loudly sounded or striked. With less load, the boat or the cart can be used for further transportation. Thus the centre is various. While the intelligence, power, shape, or sound work, the centre will be empty.（枯龟无我,能见大知;磁石无我,能见大力;钟鼓无我,能见大音;舟车无我,能见远行。故我一身,虽有智有力,有行有音,未尝有我。）

archimedes law（阿基米德定律）—The buoyancy equals to the weight of displaced liquid. For ships, the buoyancy of a ship equals to the weight of displaced water where the ship is located.

Sun and Mao wood structure（榫卯结构）—The word Sun（榫）and the word Mao （卯）are wood structures. The Sun is a male wood part whereas the Mao is the female wood part. Sun and Mao wood structures were widely used to build ancient palaces and houses. Sun and Mao wood structure is also interpreted as the mortise tendon connection. Sun and Mao wood structures are approaches to build large ships in ancient China. Because no nails were used in the shipbuilding, the corruptions to the nails did not exist. In that case, the safety of the ship kept to the maximum.

VI. Exercises

1. Discuss with your classmates and answer the following questions.

1）Tell us the story of Gonggu and Huodi.

2）What is the difference between Shanxi and Shannxi?

3）What is difference between the Chinese characters "筏" and "船"?

4）What does "舰" mean in old Chinese?

5）Do "舫" and "防" have similarities in meaning?

6）What are rules for names of ships on the basis of *Changshabanbo* and *Danyangchuan*?

7）Why do we call *Zhenghebaochuan* for vessels in Zhenghe's fleet?

8）Guess the meaning of *Ge* in "百舸争流".

9）Where is Yalujiang River? What ancient ship was used in it?

10）Where did *Dengguanchuan*（邓关船）sail?

2. Deep thinking.

1）Why do we use many Chinese Pinyin in the text?

2）Explain the significance of Sun and Mao.

3）Explain the Floating Theory in Chinese Philosophy and explain the significance.

4）While we see the rafts in the upstream of the Yellow River, what can we imagine?

5）What can we conclude from the names of ships in ancient times?

6）When Chinese wish to describe the borrowed thing, they use "舶来品". What are causes?

7）Choose a Chinese poem with word "舟" and "帆" and imagine the shipbuilding in that period.

8）What are functions of *Qiang* and *Lu* on the basis of "谈笑间,樯橹灰飞烟灭。"?

9）What does the Chinese character "俞" mean in *Yudaniangchuan*（俞大娘船）?

10）How are "长江" and "黄河" translated into English? Please comment.

3. Translate the following sentences into English.

1）古者共鼓、货狄,刳木为舟,剡木为楫,以济不通。

2）公元 640 年,隋炀帝杨广为了要到扬州一游,命官吏督造龙舟及杂船数十艘。杨广乘坐的大龙舟,高 45 尺,长 200 尺,上层有正殿、内殿,东西朝堂,中间两层有 120 个房间,全部用金玉装饰,还有高三层的龙舟九艘。

3）船只越大,制造工艺也就越加复杂。唐朝内河船中,长 20 余丈,载人六七百者已屡见不鲜。有的船上居然能开圃种花种菜,仅水手就达数百人之多,舟船之大可以想见。

4）唐朝舟船已采用了先进的钉接榫合的连接工艺,使船的强度大大提高。宋朝造船和修船已经开始使用船坞,这比欧洲早了 500 年。

5）郑和下西洋船队的主要船舶叫宝船,它采用的是中国古代适于远洋航行优秀船型——福船型。它高大如楼,底尖面阔,首尾高昂,首尖尾方,两侧有护板,船舱为水密隔舱结构。

4. Translate the following sentences into Chinese.

1）Shipbuilders in the Ming dynasty（1368–1644）were not the same as the shipbuilders in other Chinese dynasties, due to hundreds of years of accumulated experiences and rapid changes in the Ming dynasty. Shipbuilders in the Ming dynasty primarily worked for the government, under command of the Ministry of Public Works.

2）The ancient Chinese also built ramming vessels as in the Greco-Roman tradition of the trireme, although oar-steered ships in China lost favor very early on since it was in the 1st century China that the stern-mounted rudder was first developed. This was dually met with the introductions of the Han Dynasty junk ship design in the same century. It is thought that the Chinese had adopted the Malay junk sail by this period.

3）The naval history of China stems back to the Spring and Autumn period（722 BCE– 481 BCE）of the ancient Chinese Zhou Dynasty. The Chinese built large rectangular barges known as "castle ships", which were essentially floating fortresses complete with multiple decks with guarded ramparts. However, the Chinese vessels during this era were essentially fluvial(riverine). True ocean-going fleets did not appear until the 10th century Song Dynasty.

4）Evidence from Ancient Egypt shows that the early Egyptians knew how to assemble planks of wood into a ship hull as early as 3,100 BCE. Egyptian pottery as old as 4,000 BCE shows designs of early boats or other means for navigation. The Archaeological Institute of America reports that some of the oldest ships yet unearthed are known as the Abydos boats. These are a group of 14 ships discovered in Abydos that were constructed of wooden planks which were "sewn" together.

5）Sometime around the 12th century, northern European ships began to be built with a straight sternpost, enabling the mounting of a rudder, which was much more durable than a steering oar held over the side. Development in the Middle Ages favored "round ships", with a broad beam and heavily curved at both ends. Another important ship type was the galley which was constructed with both sails and oars.

Lesson 13   Introductions to the Shipbuilding
Administration in China
第 13 课   中国造船主管机关介绍

Under the leadership of the CPC, the shipbuilding industry becomes the world largest shipbuilding industry. There are two stages after the foundering of the People's Republic of China. The primary stage is the stage before 14th October, 2019 and the second stage is the stage after 14th October, 2019.

I. Primary Stage of Shipbuilding Administration in China

In the primary stage, there were four sub-stages, namely the stage between October 1950 and January 1953, the stage between February 1958 and August, 1963, the stage between September, 1963 and May 1982, the stage between June 1982 and June 1999, and the stage between July 1999 and October 2019.

On 1st October, 1950, the Shipbuilding Bureau under the Ministry of Heavy Industry was founded. In January, 1953, the Shipbuilding Bureau was shifted to No.1 Ministry of Machine Building Industry. This is the first step for shipbuilding administration in China.

In February 1958, two Ministries of Machine Building Industry joint into No.1 Ministry of Machine Building Industry. The administration of the shipbuilding industry was renamed to No.9 Industrial Management Bureau. On 13th September, 1960, the No.1 Ministry of Machine Building Industry was reorganized and separated into No.1 and No.3 Ministries of Machine Building Industry. No.9 Industrial Management Bureau was under the direction of the No.3 Ministry of Machine Building Industry.

On 17th of September, 1963, No.9 Industrial Management Bureau was reorganized as No.6 Ministry of Machine Building Industry. It ran under May, 1982.

On 4th of May, 1982, No.6 Ministry of Machine Building Industry was cancelled and China State Shipbuilding Corporation (CSSC) was established. In July, 1999, China State Shipbuilding Corporation (CSSC) and China Shipbuilding Heavy Industry Corporation (CSIC) are established instead of the original CSSC.

II. Shipbuilding Administration

Under the leadership of the CPC, the State Council carried out a reform on 14th October, 2019. The two shipbuilding corporations—China State Shipbuilding Corporation and China Shipbuilding Heavy Industry Corporation were merged as one group. It is called China

State Shipbuilding Corporation Limited and 104 main enterprises, research centres with more than 222,000 staffs are composed of it. The total property is more than 890 billions of RMB yuan and it is the largest shipbuilding industry in the world. The shipbuilding production is capable of satisfying with the needs from shipowners. It manages all state-run shipyards are in China. The shipyards include, for example, Dalian Shipbuilding Industry Company Limited, Bohai Shipbuilding Heavy Industry Company Limited, Guangzhou Huangpu Shipbuilding Company Limited, Guangzhou Shipyard International Company Limited, Jiangxi Shipbuilding Company Limited, Shanghai Waigaoqiao Shipbuilding Company Limited, Hudong-Zhonghua Shipbuilding (Group) Company Limited , Wuhu Shipyard Company Limited, etc.

In addition to the state-run shipbuilding companies attached to the CSSC, COSCO SHIPPING also manages a group of state-run shipbuilding companies. COSCO SHIPPING was established in December, 2016. The headquarters is located in Shanghai. It owns 9 large shipbuilding companies. In addition to the shipbuilding, the shipbuilding companies also build marine engineering parts. The manufactures cover almost all types of shipbuilding products.

Under the leadership of the CPC, shipbuilding industry in China has been becoming the first shipbuilding industry in the world. Shipbuilding industry is benefit from China making.

III. Samples of Shipbuilding Enterprises under CSSC

Dalian Shipbuilding Industry Company Limited

DSIC stands for Dalian Shipbuilding Industry Company Limited and it is operated under China State Shipbuilding Corporation Limited and DSIC is a public company that has been listed on the stock market. The headquarters is located in Dalian City. It was founded in 1898 and it becomes one of the largest shipyards in China and it is the largest shipyards in north of China. It built the first Chinese Oceangoing ships *Yuejin* on 27th of November, 1958 and it began the first voyage on April 30, 1963. In total, it built more than 820 naval ships of 44 types since the founding of the People's Republic of China and the first Chinese aircraft carrier was built in DSIC.

Hudong-Zhonghua Shipbuilding (Group) Company Limited

Hudong-Zhonghua Shipbuilding (Group) Company Limited is one of the major shipbuilding enterprises under the flag of China State Shipbuilding Corporation (CSSC). The Company consists of one headquarter in Pudong of Shanghai, and three shipyards, i.e. the main yard, Shanghai Shipyard Co. Ltd., and Shanghai Jiangnan-Changxing Shipbuilding Company Limited., being a comprehensive industrial conglomerate specialized in building ships, offshore engineering products and non-ship products. The production is mainly carried out in Pudong, Puxi, Changxing Island and Chongming Island of Shanghai. Besides, the Company has also interest-controlled many businesses, boasting a complete set of marine equipment fabrication industrial chains. It is one of the largest shipyards in China.

Shanghai Waigaoqiao Shipbuilding Company Limited

SWS is short for Shanghai Waigaoqiao Shipbuilding Company Limited and it was founded in 1999. It is a wholly owned subsidiary of China CSSC Holding Ltd., which means it is a publicly listed company controlled by China State Shipbuilding Corporation Limited (CSSC). It entirely owns Shanghai Waigaoqiao Shipbuilding and Offshore Company Limited. SWS Offshore, controls Shanghai Waigaoqiao Shipbuilding & Offshore Engineering Company Limited (SWS Engineering), and shares the CSSC Cruise Technology Development Company Limited (CCTD). It has been one of the most large-scale, modernized, professional and influential shipbuilding enterprises in the industry. It can make all types of ships.

Jiangsu Yangzijiang Shipbuilding Group Limited

It is a large enterprise group with shipbuilding and offshore as our core business, trade logistics, ship-leasing and real estate as supplementary business. The group owns Jiangsu New Yangzi Shipbuilding Company Limited , Jiangsu Yangzi Xinfu Shipbuilding Company Limited, Jiangsu Yangzi-Mitsui Shipbuilding Company Limited, and Jiangsu Yangzijiang Shipbuilding Company Limited, which are located on the golden waterway and lower reaches of the Yangtze River, nearby the cities of Jingjiang, Jiangyin, Taixing and Taicang, in Jiangsu province, around 170 km away either to Shanghai or Nanjing.

Guangzhou Wenchong Shipyard Company Limited

GWS is short for Guangzhou Wenchong Shipyard Company Limited. It is located in south-east of Guangzhou, between Huangpu old and new Ports. It is a large state-owned enterprise, an important enterprise under the CSSC in the south of China. GWS has very convenience communication environment. It was founded in 1955 and reformed into a limited company in 2001. It mainly engages in building container vessels & dredgers, installation and manufacture for ports machinery, metallic structure & parts, etc.

Nantong COSCO KHI Ship Engineering Company Limited

NACKS is short for Nantong COSCO KHI Ship Engineering Company Limited. It is the first large-scale Sino-foreign joint venture shipbuilding enterprise in China established by COSCO SHIPPING Group and Kawasaki Heavy Industries Company Limited (short as "KHI"). The company has a registered capital of 1.46 billion RMB Yuan and a total investment of over 6 billion Yuan, for which COSCO SHIPPING and KHI respectively hold 50% of shares of NACKS. It is one of the largest shipyards in China and it is located in Nantong City, Jiangsu Province.

COSCO SHIPPING Shipyard Group Company Limited

The COSCO SHIPPING Shipyard Group Company Limited was founded in June 2001 and it is a subsidiary of COSCO SHIPPING. It is a large enterprise group, specializing in large vessels building, marine engineering's construction and conversion, and providing with services in ship repairing and building sets. It is located in Ganjingzi District, Dalian City. It is one of the largest shipbuilding companies in China.

Dalian COSCO SHIPPING and KHI Ship Engineering Company Limited

DACKS stands for Dalian COSCO SHIPPING and KHI Ship Engineering Company Limited. It was jointly invested by China COSCO SHIPPING Corporation Limited (COSCO SHIPPING) and Kawasaki Heavy Industries, Ltd. (KHI) on July 18, 2007. The company is located in Developing Zone Lvshunkou District, Dalian City.

IV. Related Culture Words and Technical Terms

shipbuilding (造船)—It is the construction of ships and other floating vessels. It normally takes place in a specialized facility known as a shipyard. Shipbuilders, also called shipwrights, follow a specialized occupation that traces its roots to before recorded history.

heavy industry (重工业)—It is an industry that involves one or more characteristics such as large and heavy products; large and heavy equipment and facilities (such as heavy equipment, large machine tools, huge buildings and large-scale infrastructure); or complex or numerous processes. Because of those factors, heavy industry involves higher capital intensity than light industry does, and it is also often more heavily cyclical in investment and employment.

Made in China, 2025 (中国制造 2025)—It is a plan made in May 2015. It is planned to achieve the strong manufacturing country in 2025. Those also include the shipbuilding industry as the shipbuilding is one of the heavy industries.

Shipbuilding Administration (造船主管机关)—It is the top administration to guide the shipbuilding in all aspects. In China, the CSSC is the sole administration to guide the state run shipbuilding.

The leadership of the CPC (中国共产党领导) in the shipbuilding —The shipbuilding is the mainstream of the heavy industry in the country. The Communist Party of China guides the activities in all aspects of the shipbuilding industry, as the CPC is the core leadership for the cause of Chinese socialism. The achievement of shipbuilding in China proves that the leadership of the CPC is the only way to achieve the success.

Cares from the CPC, Administrations, Working Unions, League Communities (党政工团关怀)—It is a socialistic system to care staffs in the shipbuilding industry. In China, all organisations, unions cooperate in order to harmonise the working systems and the society. It embodies that socialism is much better than the capitalism.

Great Craftman Spirit (大国工匠精神)—To foster the skillful craftmen in shipbuilding. For instance, welding workers do the firmed welding works in order to guarantee the qualities of the shipbuilding. The Great Craftman Spirit is the soul which shipbuilders try to pursue.

V. Exercises

1. Discuss with your classmates and answer the following questions.

1）What were "南船" and "北船"?

2）Which company built the first Chinese oceangoing ship? What is the name of the ship?

3）What is the relationship between NACKS and DACKS?

4）Please list top 3 largest shipyard in China.

5）How many staffs are there in the CSSC now?

6）List the top 3 countries in shipbuilding.

7）When did the first Shipbuilding Administration set up in China?

8）In our daily life, we may describe Shanghai as Great Shanghai. Please describe shipbuilding companies in Shanghai.

9）What does the word "headquarters" mean? Is it singular or plural?

10）Can you make a difference between the heavy industry and the light industry? Please discuss the concept. Can you make a comment on new terms to describe those?

2. Deep thinking.

1）Although the shipbuilding organization changes due to the reform, Chinese shipbuilding has become the world No.1. Explain the causes.

2）Explain the significance of the leadership of the CPC in the shipbuilding industry.

3）In China, the care project is effective. Here the care project refers to cares from CPC, administration, working union, and league party. Explain the significance in running the shipbuilding industry.

4）In the 1980s, Japanese shipbuilding used to be the world No.1. In the 1990s and 2000s, shipbuilding in the Republic of Korea used to be the world No.1. Nowadays, China becomes the world No.1. Please explain the causes.

5）Describe the relationships between China Manufacturing and China Shipbuilding.

6）Check the sites of shipyard and explain the similarities.

7）Why is there no shipyard in the banks of the Yellow River?

8）Why does the shipbuilding belong to the heavy industry?

9）Please describe the shipbuilding status in Jiangsu, Zhejiang, and Shanghai. Explain those shipyards there.

10）Do you think the artificial intelligence is able to be used in the shipbuilding industry?

3. Translate the following sentences into English.

1）造船人有着一股不服输的韧劲,中华人民共和国成立初期旧中国留给我们的是一穷二白。造船人自主建厂,经过几十年的不懈努力,中国造船业目前走在世界的前列。

2）中国船舶集团有限公司是按照党中央决策,由国务院批准。2019 年 10 月 14 日由原中国船舶工业集团有限公司与原中国船舶重工集团有限公司联合重组成立的特大型国有重要骨干企业。

3）中国船舶集团有限公司能够设计建造符合全球船级社规范、满足国际通用技术标准和安全公约要求的船舶海工装备,是全球最大的造船集团。

4）中国船舶集团董事会,是决策机构,对国务院国资委负责,依法行使职权。中国船舶集团经理层是执行机构,按照规定执行董事会决议,开展生产经营工作。

5）中国船舶集团有限公司是我国船舶工业发展的国家队、主力军,坚持走自力更生、自主创新发展道路,培育了超大型智能化油船、液化天然气运输船、超大型集装箱船等集研发、制造、配套为一体的世界级海洋装备先进产业集群,不断向全球产业链和价值链高端延伸,引领我国由世界第一造船大国走向造船强国,为我国经济社会发展和全球海事业发展做出了重要贡献。

4. Translate the following sentences into Chinese.

1）A shipyard（also called a dockyard）is a place where ships are built and repaired. These can be yachts, military vessels, cruise liners or other cargo or passenger ships. Dockyards are sometimes more associated with maintenance and basing activities than shipyards, which are sometimes associated more with initial construction. The terms are routinely used interchangeably, in part because the evolution of dockyards and shipyards has often caused them to change or merge roles.

2）The site of a large shipyard will contain many specialised cranes, dry docks, slipways, dust-free warehouses, painting facilities and extremely large areas for fabrication of the ships. After a ship's useful life is over, it makes its final voyage to a shipbreaking yard, often on a beach in South Asia. Historically shipbreaking was carried on in drydock in developed countries, but high wages and environmental regulations have resulted in movement of the industry to developing regions.

3）It was recorded that the world's earliest known dockyards were built in the Harappan port city of Lothal circa 2,600 BCE in Gujarat, India. Lothal's dockyards connected to an ancient course of the Sabarmati river on the trade route between Harappan cities in Sindh and the peninsula of Saurashtra when the surrounding Kutch desert was a part of the Arabian Sea.

4）Shipyards are constructed near the sea or tidal rivers to allow easy access for their ships. The United Kingdom, for example, has shipyards on many of its rivers. The site of a large shipyard will contain many specialised cranes, dry docks, slipways, dust-free warehouses, painting facilities and extremely large areas for fabrication of the ships.

5）The name of the ancient Greek city of Naupactus means "shipyard". Naupactus' reputation in this field extends to the time of legend, where it is depicted as the place where the Heraclidae built a fleet to invade the Peloponnesus. In the Spanish city of Barcelona, the Drassanes shipyards were active from at least the mid-13th century until the 18th century, although it at times served as a barracks for troops as well as an arsenal. During its time of operation it was continuously changed, rebuilt and modified, but two original towers and part of the original eight construction naves remain today. It is currently a maritime museum.

Lesson 14   Introductions to Shipbuilding
第 14 课　船舶建造介绍

The shipbuilding is a heavy industry involving large co-operations from material preparations to organization handlings. The shipyard facilities will be used and the technical staffs and workers of the shipyard will participate in.

I . Shipbuilding Contract

The Shipowner will sign a contract with the shipyard after a long time study. The Shipowner may consider the shipbuilding quality, the reputations of the shipyard, the capabilities of the shipbuilding, time for the shipbuilding, budget, etc. After making the shipbuilding contract, the shipbuilding process will start. In general, the General Chief Engineer is the top leader of the shipbuilding under the direction of the General Manager or the CEO. The Technical Support Department is the department to take charge of the shipbuilding programme. Upon the signature of the Shipbuilding Contract, the Technical Support Department is responsible for carrying out the shipbuilding project.

II . Shipbuilding Procedure

The contract will be made between the Shipowner and the Shipyard and then the shipbuilding procedure is in progress. The entire procedure includes drawing designs, plan approval, plan issue, steel ordering, loft work, numerical control, shipyard layout, material handling, material preparation, shot-blasted and priming, straightening, cutting and shaping, outfitting, sea trial, delivery, etc. We can choose important step to explain.

The beginning of the shipbuilding is the ship design. The drawing office or even the ship research centre will design a ship to satisfy the requirements of the Shipowner. In this stage, a Superintendent (SI) from the Shipowner and the Classification Society for the new ship will join in. The designers will amend the drawings to meet requirements of the Shipowner and the Classification Society. As soon as the drawings have been approved, the plans will be sent to the relevant parties for reference. The shipbuilding is on the way.

The next step is the preparation of materials. In other words, the steel will be ordered for the shipbuilding. It is essential to prepare the materials before the shipbuilding. In general, there are huge stores in the Shipyard. The qualified steel will be delivered to the Shipyard for shipbuilding. In general, the Shipyard shall cooperate with Steel Manufacturers and the Steel

Manufacturers will offer the qualified steel to the Shipyard. The quality of the steel is essential and the steel has been verified before using.

Then the lofting work is necessary. As a general rule, the loft work for the new ship takes place in a mould loft. The mould loft will be stowed in a large covered area with a wooden floor upon which the ship's details are drawn to the full size or some smaller comfortable size. In recent years, the lofting work has been done by the software of computer. However very significant locations still require the real lofting work.

The next step is the numerical control. A numerical control system is one where a machine is operated and controlled by the insertion of numerical data. The numerical data is a sequence of numbers which fully describe a part to be produced. Moreover, the use of certain code numbers enables instructions to be fed into the machine to enable it to operate automatically. A reading device on the machine converts the numbers into electrical impulses which become control signals for the various parts of the machine which produce the finished part.

The shipyard layout is the real beginning of the shipbuilding. The shipyard layout is arranged to provide a logical ordered flow of materials and equipment towards the final units build-up, erection and outfitting of the ship. The various production stages are arranged in work areas or "shops" and, as far as practicable in modern yards, take place under cover, the sequence of events is as follows, preliminary ship design, drawing of detailed plans, approval of plans and issue, loft work and production of table of offsets, issue of steel and production beginning, material preparation—shot-blastion and priming, manufacturer of plates and sections—marking, cutting, machining and shaping, subassemblies and assemblies produced, units fabricated and delivered to the berth, and units erected faired and welded.

The materials handing is the next step. The layout of a shipyard is aimed to reduced materials handling to a minimum by appropriate location of work stations or areas. The building of large units and the capacity to transport them will reduce the number of items handled but will require great care and more sophisticated equipment. The building of a ship is as much governed by the shipyard layout as the materials handling equipment and its capacity.

The material preparation will then be in progress. Plates and sections received from the steel mill are shot-blasted to remove scale, primed with a temporary protective paint and finally straightened by rolls to remove any curvature. Shot-blasted and priming are also essential. A typical machine will first water-wash then heat-dry the plates before descaling. The plates are then simultaneously shot-blasted both sides with metallic abrasive. Blowers and suction devices remove the shot which is cleaned and recycled. The clean plate are immediately covered with a coat of priming paint and dried in an automatic spraying machine.

The straightening is a shaping process. The plate straightening or leveling is achieved by using a plate rolls machine. This consists of five large rollers, the bottom two being driven and the top ones idling. The top rollers can be adjusted for height independently at each end and the bottom rollers have adjustable centres. A number of smaller supporting rollers are positioned around the five main rollers. The plate is fed through with the upper and lower rollers spaced at its thickness and is subsequently straightened. This machine is also capable of bending and flanging plate.

Cutting and shaping

Various machines and equipment are used for cutting and shaping the steel parts which form the subassemblies, assemblies, and units.

A sea trial will be completed prior to delivery. The sea trial is the procedure to determine manoeuvring data. The problem may be found in the sea trial and adjustment will be done after sea trial.

The naming or christening will be the important process in the shipbuilding. The ship will be named by an important person from the Shipowner. In western countries, the person who names the ship is called Godmother. The person must be a female and she is chosen by the Shipowner. The naming is called christening in western countries. In China, we use name the ship in Chinese tradition. We just call to name a ship. Sometimes ship naming and delivery are arranged together.

III. Related Culture Words and Technical Terms

lofting (*n.*) (放样)—It is a drafting technique (sometimes using mathematical tables) whereby curved lines are generated, and it is to be used in plans for stream lined objects such as aircraft and boats. The lines may be drawn on wood and the wood then cut for advanced wood working. The technique can be as simple as bending a flexible object, such as along strip of thin wood or thin plastic so that it passes over three non-linear points, and scribing the resultant curved line; or as elaborate splitting the line using computers or mathematical tables.

outfitting (*n.*) (舾装)—To decorate a ship after shipbuilding. The ship is just in a frame after building. It is necessary to outfit after building. Those include the installation of stairs, windows, and side scuttles, decorations of cabins, etc. Outfitting looks like decoration of rooms in the real estate.

launching (*n.*) (下水)—The launching is a procedure to let the ship launch in the water. It is the first time that the entire the water. There are different methods or approaches to let the ship launch into the water, for example, gravity launching, floating launching, pulling launching. In accordance with the directions of launching, the launching methods or approaches are divided into transverse launching and longitudinal launching.

sea trial (海试)—The sea trial is a necessary procedure to test the parameters, measurements, or the particulars in order to test the quality of the shipbuilding. In general, the ship will be adjusted as soon as the problems are found in the sea trial. The sea trial may be executed several times if necessary.

IV. Exercises

1. Discuss with your classmates and answer the following questions.

1）What is the abbreviation SI short for?

2）In the shipping company, which department is responsible for the shipbuilding?

3）In the shipping company, which department is responsible for the shipbuilding budget?

4）Do you think the shipbuilder is able to make steel for the shipbuilding? Why or why not?

5）Who will offer the building materials for the shipyard?

6）Why do we use computer lofting instead of traditional lofting?

7）What is the difference between naming and delivery?

8）Describe the facilities and equipment used for shipbuilding.

9）What does the term General Chief Engineer mean? Does he or she work on board?

10）What is the difference between CEO and general manager?

2. Deep thinking.

1）What is the relationship among the Shipbuilder, the Shipowner, and the Ship Surveyor?

2）Why is the Superintendent arranged on behalf of the Shipowner?

3）Why do we use the term "naming" instead of "christening"?

4）How do you comprehend the term "outfitting"?

5）What is the motivation of the shipbuilding?

6）When shipbuilding is deemed as a type of heavy industry, what will the landscape in your mind?

7）Why must a bottle of champagne be broken in the ceremony of the launching? What is the tradition?

8）Why is the ship design is important?

9）Why is the computer significant in the shipbuilding?

10）Why should the shipyard prepare the building material before shipbuilding?

3. Translate the following sentences into English.

1）重力式下水又分纵向滑道涂油式下水、纵向钢珠滑道下水、横向涂油滑道下水等方式。

2）漂浮式下水是指用水泵或以自流方式将水注入造船的船坞内，当水注满后船舶自动漂浮。

3）线性放样分手工放样和机器放样。手工放样通常是按照 1：1 比例，样台需要占用极大的面积，需要大量的人力、物力，目前很少使用。机器放样通过电脑模拟可以做到，目前被广泛采用。

4）开始造船时，船级社就已经介入，船级社会根据船东要求的船型给出非常专业的建议，造船机构根据船级社的建议改进船舶设计。

5）对于船舶命名我们使用"命名"一词，因为命名本身就是应该遵守唯物主义思想，命名没有宗教色彩，船舶安全靠船舶建造质量和船员的安全操作。

4. Translate the following sentences into Chinese.

1）Shipbuilding is the construction of ships and other floating vessels. It normally takes place in a specialized facility known as a shipyard. Shipbuilders, also called shipwrights, follow a specialized occupation that traces its roots to before recorded history.

2）Shipbuilding and ship repairs, both commercial and military, are referred to as "naval engineering". The construction of boats is a similar activity called boat building. The dismantling of ships is called ship breaking.

3）The oldest known tidal dock in the world was built around 2500 BCE during the Harappan civilisation at Lothal near the present day Mangrol harbour on the Gujarat coast in India. Other ports were probably at Balakot and Dwark.

4）Dockyards are sometimes more associated with maintenance and basing activities than shipyards, which are sometimes associated more with initial construction. The terms are routinely used interchangeably, in part because the evolution of dockyards and shipyards has often caused them to change or merge roles.

5）The site of a large shipyard will contain many specialised cranes, dry docks, slipways, dust-free warehouses, painting facilities and extremely large areas for fabrication of the ships. After a ship's useful life is over, it makes its final voyage to a shipbreaking yard, often on a beach in South Asia.

Lesson 15　Introductions to Ship Repairs
第 15 课　船舶维修介绍

The ship repair or refit is an approach to keep the ship in good working order in the process of servicing. In common practice, the ship may suffer from wear and tear in her running, she even suffer from a damage caused by the accident. For example, a ship was damaged after colliding with another ship or shore facilities. In that case, the ship needs to be repaired.

Ⅰ. Types of Ship Repairs

The ship repair may be divided into the running repair, the current repair, and the extensive repair. The running repair, as the name suggests, is a repair while the ship is in normal transport service. That is the case when the ship suffered from minor damage. The repairers from the shipyard will be employed to repair her while she is still running for transportation. The current repair is also called annual repair. It is a kind of docking repair for deficiency rectifications found in the intermediate survey or an annual survey. The Surveyors may recommend the repair regarding the survey and therefore the ship will be arranged for repair in accordance with the recommendations. The extensive repair is the largest scale repair amongst all repairs. Normally the ship will be arranged for the extensive repair after 2 or 3 annual repairs. In other words, the ship is required for the extensive repair within 4 to 6 years. The exceptional repair is the damage repair, which means the ship is repaired after an accident.

Ⅱ. Descriptions of the Repair List

The Repair List is the basically technical documents to embody the repair requirements on behalf of the Shipowner. It may include the content of the repair, the extent of the repair, and the requirements of the repair. It is also the basis for the shipyard to estimate the work hour, make the budget, and finally sign the Repair Contract. For the Technical Support Department of the Shipowner, it is the basis to arrange the Repair Plan for the ship and to make a practical and economical budget. The original Repair List is made by the ship to be repaired. The Shipmaster, the Chief Officer, and other Deck Officers, the Chief Engineer, other Marine Engineers, and the ETO should investigate the status of the ship and collect all feedbacks in accordance with the drawbacks and deficiencies in the operation for her. They should get familiar with the running conditions of the critical equipment. All crewmembers are required to take part in self-checking work under the instructions from the Shipmaster, Officers, and Engineers. They will collect all items and make a draft Repair List. The Engineers from the Technical Support Department of the Shipowner will then decide the self-repair items and repair items for the shipyard.

Ⅲ. Descriptions of the Repair Bill

The Repair Bill is a legal document made by the General Chief Engineer or the responsible staff of the Technical Support Department, the Chief Accountant of the Financial Department, and the responsible Deputy Manager or even the General Manager. They will take the budget and number and extents of the repair items into consideration. On the basis of the Repair List, the Shipowner will make a Repair Bill, the Repair List and the Repair Bill are used for negotiation with the Engineers from the shipyard. The Repair Contract will be made on the basis of the Repair List and the Repair Bill. The shipyard Engineers or the shipyard Accountant will also verify and calculate the expenses, including the materials used in the repair, the work hours, and marginal benefits, etc. They will then make a Repair Contract with the Shipowner. The Repair Bill and the Repair List will be attached to the Repair Contract.

Ⅳ. Related Culture Words and Technical Terms

SI (*n.*) (superintendent, 监督)—It is a name for the person nominated by the Shipowner to monitor and control the ship operations including ship repair.

breakdown (*n.*) (分项报价)—It is a term used in shipping industry to show the total items are to be broken down into sub-items.

lump sum (一揽子,总和)—It is upset to the term breakdown. It is especially used in the budgets, payments or some areas related to the money.

surveillance system (监督系统)—It is a monitoring system in the ship repair. In general, the Superintendent, the Shipmaster, Deck Officers and Engineers, deck hands and engine hands will monitor the entire repair work on spot in order to control the repair quality.

joint inspections before repair (维修前的联合检查)—In general, the engineers and the responsible person from the shipyard and the shipowner's staff will jointly check the ship before the work to check all repair items and some specifications before working.

on squatting (坐坞)—In general, the ship will repair the bottom after entering the dock in the shipyard. The ship will squat onto the berth and the water will be drained out. That is the procedure for dry-docking.

Ⅴ. Exercises

1. Discuss with your classmates and answer the following questions.

1) What does the term Annual Repair mean?

2）What does the term Damage Repair mean?

3）What does the term Major Repair mean?

4）What does the term Minor Repair mean?

5）Who takes charge of the repair work in the Engine Department?

6）Who takes charge of the repair work in the Deck Department?

7）Who takes charge of the repair work in the Shipping Company?

8）What is the word difference between dock and docking?

9）What does the term emergency repair mean?

10）What does the term voyage repair mean?

2. Deep thinking.

1）How can you make differences between the word repair and refit?

2）Why is the Superintendent arranged for the repair work?

3）What is the difference between the Repair List and the Repair Bill?

4）Why are the recommendations from the Surveyors important in the repair?

5）What is called the quality of repair in your opinion?

6）If the Shipowner asks to add new repair items, will the Shipyard agree? Why or why not?

7）Why does a ship need maintenance and repair?

8）How will you monitor the repair quality as a Chief Officer?

9）What safety measures will be taken for the painting work?

10）Whose decision will be the final if the Captain's decision is contradictory with the Superintendent?

3. Translate the following sentences into English.

1）驾驶台需要安装电子式天文钟,型号应该按照修船单上规定型号提供。

2）大副舱室的空调散热片损坏,房间送冷气时,温度不下降,需要修理。

3）2号货舱海水冷却管应放至货舱外,因为舱内冷却会积水,导致货物发霉。

4）在总管的法兰盘附近有两处漏点,一处在锅炉上方,另一处在机舱门上方,此管路需要换新。

5）驾驶台左舷舷窗挂钩坏了,需要换新。此外窗帘也需要换新,尺寸按照原窗帘的尺寸做。

4. Translate the following sentences into Chinese.

1）The bottom area from the keel to light loadline approximate 1,724 square metres with high pressure fresh water. The rusted area to be cleaned by disc sanding or wire rushing and to be touched up one coat of A/C and A/F paint.

2）Both bow anchors and chains of lengths in total to be ranged in dock. Both side anchor cable shackles to be remarked with new stainless wires seizing and mark with white paint, and then anchor and chains to be readjusted properly.

3）Item 477 E/R tank top painting—Tank top to be cleaned with chemicals or oil detergent. Result to be shown and approved by the Shipowner. Item 488 M/E scavenging coolers cleaning system—Missing, hoses and couplings to be supplied. Item 496 CP propeller—Wrong way alarm according to St. Lawrence Regulations, to be fitted on the bridge.

4) Item 0613—The rudder in the starboard lifeboat broken. Item 0830—Wire in the emergency generator cabin exposed. Item 0938—Side shell deformed/fractures in hatch coaming No. 2. Item 0630—Launching device malfunction and the limit switches of the lifeboat are in poor condition.

5) In general, there are some marks on spot before working. Those marks are used for the relative reasons. For example, crewmembers may leave the marks to remind the shipyard workers the repair items on spot. Alternatively, the Shipyard Engineer may use marks to remind the shipyard workers.

Lesson 16　Introductions to Marine Engineering Projects
第16课　海洋工程介绍

The Marine Engineering is a type of large work for the purpose of exploitation and use ocean resources. There are three types, namely coastal engineering, offshore engineering, and deep-water offshore engineering.

I. Introductions to Types of Marine Engineering Projects

Coastal Engineering: The coastal engineering is a project located in the vicinity of the coast. It may include breakwater building, reclamation project, harbour building, estuary clearance, off-shore dredging service, fishery facility building, and environmental protection of near coast, etc.

Offshore Engineering: The offshore engineering is located on the shelf of the continent. It was developed since the middle of 20th century. The engineering includes building of mobile offshore drilling unit, artificial island building, mobile semi-submersible unit, self-elevating unit, floating production, storage and offloading (FPSO) facilities, floating refinery quay, floating airport, etc.

Deep-water Offshore Engineering: It includes several engineering programs in deep-water off-shore engineering, for instance, the unmanned submarine and remote control mining facilities onto the seabed of the deep-water.

The operations at the deep water are the most difficult among all ocean engineering projects, since it is difficult to control wind, sea current, tide, icy situation, etc. It is also difficult to visually watch the operation underwater.

II. Descriptions of Marine Engineering Projects

To build a cross-sea bridge is a marine engineering project, and a cross-sea bridge is a large and long bridge going across two coasts. At beginning of the building, the buildings of underwater foundations are crucial. Very huge concretes were built on shore and those will be sunk at the predetermined locations. Piling services are important. The bases were impacted into the rocks to fix the foundations. The concretes were poured under reaching definite heights. Pier table, caisson for the bridge pier, nose of the pier, breakwater, pier coping will be established. In general, the horizontal parts were made on shore factory and those would be lifted to the prearranged locations via lifting ships. The bridge will be installed with fixing facilities and lifting ships, etc. After installation, the road on the bridge will be laid. In the process of bridge building, it is difficult to work, since the wind, current, tide, earthquake, or any other factors are to be considered.

To build a drilling platform is also a marine engineering project, and the platform is a structure that operators may stay. There are drilling facilities, power system, communication, navigation equipment, accommodation facilities, life-saving and fire-fighting equipment. There are self-rising and semi-submersible platforms. The self-rising one can rise up or lower down along the pillars in response to the tide rising and lowering. A semi-submersible platform, as the name suggests, can partially immerse into water. It is stable. In general, drill platforms were built in shipyards. The ocean-going tugs can tow the drilling platforms to the location. The platform can be lifted and squatted onto the pillars which were already piled into the seabed.

The undersea cable laying is one of key marine engineering projects. The cables include electrical power transfer and information transfer. For example, the undersea cables between East Asia and North America for signal transmissions are optical fiber cables to transmit and receive signals. They may be laid near coasts, but the lengths are much longer than the transition to the ocean. However the near coastal operations make the installations easy and the length increases are deemed as omission. Since the laying on the shelf is much easier than the laying in the mid-ocean. In general, one relay station will be installed at definite locations in order to get reliable connections and make easy maintenance. The cables will be laid on board ships and sink in the troughs. The troughs were also made by the engineering ships. In order to fix the cables precisely, the dynamic fixing approaches on board marine engineering ships are used. The most difficult work is the troughs onto the seabed, because the seabeds are different. Some seabeds are rocky and some seabeds are corals, or silt, sand. Different types of trough drilling are used to guarantee the cables are fixed while laying into the troughs.

The windmill installation in water is an important marine engineering project. A windmill is used for electricity making. As the wind is very strong at sea, the electricity made by windmill is very efficient. In general, an underwater cable will be built first and then the fixing pillar shall be made before the windmill is installed. The windmill installation is the final stage. After installation, the windmill electricity making will be commissioned.

Building underwater tunnels is also a large marine engineering project. There are four types of tunnel building, explosion, tunnel band installations, digging approaches, and shield wall constructions. The explosion method is simple, since there are rocks at the seabed. The underwater explosives are used in a large scale and the troughs will be built up and then built the troughs into the tunnel. Tunnel band installations are also simple and the tunnel bands were built on shore and then the bands were carried on board engineering ships. The bands were sunk at the predetermined locations and then the bands were connected. Digging approaches are operated by the digger ships. The rocks will be crashed and be transferred out of the operation area. Shield walls are built in order to avoid collapse. Digging operation and shield wall building are being operated at the same time. We can comprehend marine engineering operation via the samples aforementioned.

III. Related Culture Words and Technical Terms

Intelligent Marine Engineering（智慧海洋工程）—It is a name to show that marine engineering programs are on the basis of artificial intelligent.

Mobile Offshore Drilling Unit（近海移动式钻井平台）—It is a unit for exploring the oil resources underwater. As it is also a floating unit, it is deemed as a ship.

Marine Engineering Craftsmen（海洋工程工匠）—All engineers and workers who participate in the marine engineering programmes. Those staffs are significant in the marine engineering system.

The Craftsmen's Spirit（工匠精神）—It embodies the professional ethics, especially the professional ethics in the marine engineering programmes. It also embodies the professional capabilities and professional qualifications. It can prove that the devotions, contributions, and scarifications behind the craftsmen spirit.

IV. Exercises

1. Discuss with your classmates and answer the following questions.

1）What is the difference between marine engineering project（海洋工程）and marine engineering（轮机工程）?

2）What does the PFSO stand for? How is it used?

3）What is the floating refinery quay?

4）What is called seabed?

5）What is the piling vessel? When will it be used?

6）What does the abbreviation MODU stand for?

7）Why do we use cable underwater?

8）What type of companies may participate in the building of marine engineering?

9）Can you give us examples of marine engineering companies in China?

10）What is the difference between coastal engineering and offshore engineering?

2. Deep thinking.

1）Describe the importance of the bridge between Hong Kong, Zhuhai, and Macao.

2）Why does Chinese Marine Engineering lead the world?

3）Why are foundations of the bridge significant in the marine engineering programme?

4）How important of the craftsmen's spirit in the marine engineering programme?

5）What is the breakwater in a harbour? How is it used?

6）Why do we consider the earthquake factor prior to the building of a marine engineering project?

7）Why do people set up windmill installations at offshore water?

8) Why do people make use of robot for marine engineering?

9) Why do people build tunnels? Can you give us examples?

10) Why do we say diligence of Chinese helps in the marine engineering programme?

3. Translate the following sentences into English.

1) 海洋工程是指以开发、利用、保护、恢复海洋资源为目的,并且工程主体位于海岸线向海一侧的新建、改建、扩建工程。

2) 海洋工程的主要内容通常可分为资源开发技术与装备设施技术两大部分。

3) 海洋工程具体指围填海、海上堤坝工程、人工岛、海上和海底物资储藏设施、跨海桥梁、海底隧道工程等。

4) 海底管道、海底电(光)缆工程,海洋矿产资源勘探开发及其附属工程,海上潮汐电站、波浪电站也属于海洋工程的范畴。

5) 我国国家海洋主管部门对海洋工程定义,比如温差电站等海洋能源开发利用工程,大型海水养殖场,人工鱼礁工程,盐田、海水淡化等海水综合利用工程,海上娱乐及运动、景观开发工程等都属于海洋工程。

4. Translate the following sentences into Chinese.

1) Marine engineering project includes the engineering of boats, ships, oil rigs and any other marine vessel or structure, as well as oceanographic engineering, oceanic engineering or ocean engineering. Specifically, marine engineering is the discipline of applying engineering sciences, including mechanical engineering, electrical engineering, electronic engineering, and computer science, to the development, design, operation and maintenance of watercraft propulsion and on-board systems and oceanographic technology.

2) The marine engineering project also includes but is not limited to power and propulsion plants, machinery, piping, automation and control systems for marine vehicles of any kind, such as surface ships and submarines.

3) In 1712, Thomas Newcomen, a blacksmith, created a steam powered engine to pump water out of mines. In 1807, Robert Fulton successfully used a steam engine to propel a vessel through the water. Fulton's ship used the engine to power a small wooden paddle wheel as its marine propulsion system.

4) Mechanical engineers design the main propulsion plant, the powering and mechanization aspects of the ship functions such as steering, anchoring, cargo handling, heating, ventilation, air conditioning interior and exterior communication, and other related requirements. Electrical power generation and electrical power distribution systems are typically designed by their suppliers; only installation is the design responsibility of the marine engineer.

5) Anti-fouling is the process of eliminating obstructive organisms from essential components of seawater systems. Marine organisms grow and attach to the surfaces of the outboard suction inlets used to obtain water for cooling systems. Electro-chlorination involves running high electrical current through seawater. The combination of current and seawater alters the chemical composition to create sodium hypochlorite to purge any bio-matter. An

electrolytic method of anti-fouling involves running electrical current through two anodes.

Chapter Six
Shipping Logistics and Service Culture

第六章
航运物流与服务文化

本章学习目的及本章内容提要

  本章主要学习与了解航运物流特点、航运物流的工作流程、航运物流对我国乃至世界航运经济的重要影响。了解陆上运输和港口运输的对接方式，以港口为节点的物流特征，船舶交管、搜救、打捞业务特征，中国的海运物流与港口配套服务。

Lesson 17　Transport via Shore and Ports
第 17 课　通过陆地和港口运输

Transportations are various. There are different transportation all over the world. The transportation include shore-based transportation, river transportation, lake transportation, and marine transportation.

I. Road Highways for Transportation

In addition to the railway transportation, goods from China will be containerized or in bulk via trucks, lorries or other vehicles. Highways are one of transport means from the original places of the commodities to the harbour. The assembly places for the commodities may have several stages. Commodities may be collected at the first assembly place and the commodities at the first assembly places may be collected at the larger assembly places, and so forth. Then the commodities will be transported from the final assembly places to the port where the commodities are ready for transport. In China, the road connects to every corner and the road nets cover the entire country. Within five years, highways in China are increased by 534 kilometres. The highways are built in Xizang and Xinjiang where the natural environments are not suitable for road building. On the basis of the roads and highways, China has become the second largest economic body in the world under the leadership of the Communist Party of China. The roads and highways are vital for the cargo transport from the original places of the products to the loading ports and vice versa.

While the ships arrive in discharge ports, cargoes are unloaded at the discharge ports. The cargo will be carried in terms of trucks, lorries, or other vehicles. The commodities will be transferred to the final destination. The wholesalers or retailers may receive the commodities and they may sell the goods in the end markets, such as in the supermarkets.

II. Railway Transport

Railway transport from the original places of products to the ports is quite common. The large quantity of inland transportation, it is more important than the road transportation in the modern country as the speeds of the trains are much higher than other vehicles. High speed railways and bullet trains have been developing in recent years in China. Nowadays, China is the most modern country in the high speed railways and bullet trains.

III. Passenger Transferring

Passengers may choose the passenger ships or even the cruise ships for travelling. Passengers may arrive at the departure lounge of the passenger transport station at the harbour by means of different vehicles, such as shuttles, taxis, buses, or private cars. Passengers will board the ships at the designated time. If the voyage is international, the red tapes such as visa, and evidence of healthy condition shall be fulfilled by the travelling Agent.

IV. Loading Port or Port of Departure, Discharging Port or Port of Destination

The loading port is the end of the commodities at the import part. For passenger ships, the ports of departure are the starts of travelling. For cargo ships, the first ports to load cargo are the voyage starts and the export logistics is the end. The ship moving from the loading port to the discharging port is in the process of transportation. If any cargo is discharged in the middle of the voyage, the relay port is called port of call. Perhaps, there are several ports of call in one voyage, but there is only one port of origin and one port of destination. The port of destination is just the commencement of the import logistics. In short, the loading ports and discharging ports are important chains in the logistics. In the macroeconomic concept, the governments will participate in the running in terms of policy making. On the whole, the running logistics is in the background of the society, policy, and culture. The logistics includes land logistics, maritime logistics, and aviation logistics, or combined logistics, etc.

V. Related Culture Words and Technical Terms

logistics (*n.*) (物流)—In the military field it refers to the science of the movement, supplying, and maintenance of military forces in the field. In the economics, it refers to the management of materials flow through an organization, from raw materials through to finished goods.

transport (*n. & v.*) (运输)—If it is a verb, it means to move or carry (goods, for example) from one place to another; convey. It also means to cause to feel strong emotion, especially joy; carry away; enrapture. In ancient times, it also implies to send abroad to a penal colony; and deport. If it is a noun, it means that the act of transporting or conveyance. It may also imply the condition of being transported by emotion or joy or rapture. It may also refer to a ship or aircraft used to transport troops or military equipment. On the other hand, it also specifies a vehicle, such as an aircraft, used to transport passengers, mail, or freight.

economy (*n.*) (经济体)—It is a generic term for the economic activities in definite regions or areas. For example, China is the second largest economy in the world.

transportation net (交通网)—The transportation waypoints are many. The connections of the waypoints are composed of transportation lines. The combinations of transportation lines are to build up the transportation net.

transport building (交通建设)—To build transportation includes different meanings. On the broad meaning, it refers to all activities for transport. On the narrow meaning, it refers to the foundations of infrastructure for the transportation.

VI. Exercises

1. Discuss with your classmates and answer the following questions.

1) What are the top three economic bodies in the world?

2) When did China become the second largest economy in the world?

3) What vehicles run on the road transportation?

4) Can you describe some road assembly places in your hometown?

5) What is the People's Government translated?

6) How fast does the modern road increase in China?

7) Can you list transportation modes in China?

8) What does water transportation include in your opinion?

9) What types of trains do we use in China now?

10) What transportation modes are used in Xizang now?

2. Deep thinking.

1) Why do China gain the greatest economic growth within 40 years?

2) Why do we rely upon the transportation in modern society?

3) Describe the developed sub-economic bodies in China.

4) Do you think the port is the connection point in transportation net?

5) How important is the logistics in marine transportation?

6) Why should we pay attention to transportation in the building of a prosperous and modern country?

7) As an English major student, why should we learn the transportation knowledge?

8) Describe modern transportation in China now.

9) What does the green transportation mean?

10) Describe the water transportation net in China.

3. Translate the following sentences into English.

1) 轨道交通是指运营车辆需要在特定轨道上行驶的一类交通工具或运输系统。换言之,通常以电能为动力,采取轮轨运转方式的快速大运量公共交通的总称。

2) 城市交通是指在城市(包括市区和郊区)道路(地面、地下、高架、水道、索道等)系统中进行的公众出行和客货输送等。

3) 交通网是交通节点,线即连接点与点的铁路、公路、水路以及空路(航线)的交通路线。它是陆路交通、水陆交通、空中交通的总称。它也是连接纽带。

4) 水运主要承担大数量、长距离的运输,是在干线运输中起主力作用的运输形式。在内河及沿海,水运也常作为小型运输工具使用,担任补充及衔接大批量干线运输的任务。

5) 公路运输(highway transportation)是在公路上运送旅客和货物的运输方式,是交通运输系统的组成部分之一,主要承担短途客货运输。现代所用运输工具主要是汽车。

4. Translate the following sentences into Chinese.

1）Logistics is the science of planning and carrying out the movement and maintenance of forces. In its most comprehensive sense, those aspects of military operations that deal with: a. design and development, acquisition, storage, movement, distribution, maintenance, evacuation, and disposition of materiel; b. movement, evacuation, and hospitalization of personnel; c. acquisition or construction, maintenance, operation, and disposition of facilities; and d. acquisition or furnishing of services.

2）Transport means the approaches which move or copy from one location to another. It is similar with the word "transfer". In the physical world, "to transport" means "to move" (take this from here and put it there). In the electronic world, "to transport" means "to copy" the data to another location.

3）The economy is the system of production relations in any mode of production. The determining relations in this system are those pertaining to the ownership of the means of production and the character and social means of linkage between the direct producers and the means of production. The aggregate of production relations of a given mode of production is expressed in the corresponding system of economic laws and categories of political economy.

4）The process of moving cargo from place to place using more than one method of transport-truck, rail, plane, ship or any combination of those. It is similar to intermodal transport, but with multimodal transport, the shipper works with one carrier (called the "Multimodal Transport Operator" or MTO), who arranges the entire journey by all modes. The single carrier contracts with other carriers to move the freight by various modes end-to-end.

5）A mode of transport is a solution that makes use of a particular type of vehicle, infrastructure, and operation. The transport of a person or of cargo may involve one mode or several of the modes, with the latter case being called inter-modal or multi-modal transport. Each mode has its own advantages and disadvantages and will be chosen on the basis of cost, capability, and route.

Lesson 18　VTS, SAR, and Salvage Services
第 18 课　船舶交管、搜救、打捞业务

VTS, SAR, and salvage services are rendered from shore-side support or units at sea. They play a significant role in the marine shipping industry. The services may form parts of shipping culture.

Ⅰ. Introductions to the VTS

The term VTS stands for Vessel Traffic Service. It is a marine traffic monitoring and assisting system offered by the port authorities. The VTS services are rendered under IMO Assembly A. 857(20).

The IMO defines the VTS as "a service implemented by a competent authority designed to improve the safety and efficiency of vessel traffic and protect the environment. The service shall have the capability to interact with the traffic and respond to traffic situations developing in the VTS area". In general, a standard VTS system includes antenna, radar, CCTV, VHF, and AIS in order to render VTS services for all shipping. The coastal countries or regions may also be required to offer competent VTS operators to serve the services under the relevant guidelines from the IMO. The VTS services may include the control of traffic flow, providing the information service for marine shipping and receiving the arrival report and departure report, etc.

Ⅱ. Introductions to the SAR

SAR is the abbreviation for Search and Rescue. It is a SAR service in order to make provisions to assist the shipping in distress under the SAR convention. The coastal countries or regions shall establish the maritime rescue coordination centre for the purpose of offering SAR service. The countries or regions shall also provide competent personnel in order to provide the SAR service. In general, the SAR operators in the MRCC shall keep 24-hour round watch.

Nowadays, China MRCC is under the leadership of the Emergency Office of the Ministry of Transport. It is responsible for marine SAR operations as well as major maritime pollution control operations. It is also responsible for setting SAR rules as well as control rules of marine pollution. The telephone number of China MRCC is 12395.

III. Introductions to Salvage Operation

In common sense, the salvage operation is related to the SAR operation. However, they are different. In general, the SAR operation is for the shipping in distress. On the other hand, the salvage operation is the service for picking up wrecks. The salvage operation is based on the commercial basis, but the SAR operation is based on the humanitarianism. The salvage operation will merely be performed under the Salvage Contract. In China, there are three state-run salvage companies, namely Yantai Salvage Company, Shanghai Salvage Company, and Guangzhou Salvage Company. In general, they operate in the North of China, the East of China, and the South of China.

IV. Related Culture Words and Technical Terms

humanitarianism (*n.*)（人道主义）—In maritime SAR service, all assistances will be free of charge. It embodies the humanitarianism.

LOF —Lloyd's Open Form is a popular form of the salvage contract. It has been used for more than a century and it has been amended regularly in order to meet the use requirements.

Dutch merchant ship *Vergulde* —The story tells one of the world's earliest well-documented SAR efforts ensued the 1656 wreck. As the name of the wreck's *Vergulde*, it got the name of the title.

no cure, no pay（无效则无偿）—It is a term in the salvage contract. It means the salvage is in vain, the owner of the wreck will not be responsible for paying. Only if the salvage is effective, the contract for salvage fee-paying will be performed.

H24—The operation will be kept on the basis of 24 hours daily and 7 days a week. H24 means the watch will be kept continuously without disruption.

VTS traffic image —The surface picture of vessels and their movements in a VTS area.

VTS Administration —It is the top-level government office to take charge of the VTS operations. In China, VTS operations are under the management of China MSA of the Ministry of Transport.

shall (*v.*)（须）—It is used to indicate a provision, the uniform application of which by Parties is required in the interest of the safety of life at sea.

should (*v.*)（应）—It is used to indicate a provision, the uniform application of which by all Parties is recommended in the interest of safety of life at sea.

coast watching unit（海岸值守单位）—A land unit, stationary or mobile, designated to maintain a watch on the safety of vessels in coastal areas.

ditch (*v.*)（迫降）—In the case of an aircraft, to make a forced landing on water.

V. Exercises

1. Discuss with your classmates and answer the following questions.

1) What does the VTS stand for?

2) What does the VHF stand for?

3) What does the SAR stand for?

4) Please describe the facilities used in the VTS.

5) What does ditch mean in SAR convention?

6) What does the LOF for salvage operation mean?

7) What is the telephone number for maritime SAR operation in China?

8) What does IMO Assembly A. 857(20) concern?

9) Where are headquarters of Beihai Rescue Bureau, Donghai Rescue Bureau, and Nanhai Rescue Bureau in China?

10) Where are headquarters of Yantai Salvage Company, Shanghai Salvage Company, and Guangzhou Salvage Company?

2. Deep thinking

1) What does the CCTV stand for? How will you make differences between one abbreviation with different meanings?

2) In the SAR convention, "shall" and "should" are very different in meanings. How will you translate the two verbs in context?

3) What does competent authority mean?

4) What is the difference between the VTS and the VTC?

5) What is the orientation of humanitarianism?

6) What do emergency phase, uncertainty phase, and alert phase stand for?

7) What is the purpose of maritime search and rescue?

8) What does coordination in the SAR mean?

9) Can you tell us the service differences between Donghai Rescue Bureau and Shanghai Rescue Company?

10) Why do we say the Socialism concept is significant in the guidance of coordinated SAR?

3. Translate the following sentences into English.

1)船舶交管值班员需要连续值班,通常是三个班次,每次值班时值班员需要在工作岗位上进行海上交通指挥、发布海上安全信息。

2)我国海上搜救体系充分体现了社会主义的"一方有难、八方支援"的原则,为全球海上搜救体系贡献了中国方案。

3)打捞作业是根据打捞合同,对于水下沉船、水下其他物品等进行打捞的作业。打捞作业和人员救助有着明显的不同,打捞作业是有偿作业。

4)打捞作业秉承的原则是"无效则无偿",就是说打捞局无论做到了多大的努力,花费有多少,如果没有打捞出相关物品,则乙方不予补偿,除非另有约定。

5）我国交通运输部海上搜救中心与交通运输部应急办公室合署办公,负责部分应急管理日常工作和应急总值班工作;负责部分应急信息统计、分析等工作,履行应急值守、信息汇总、综合协调、对外联系等职责。

4. Translate the following sentences into Chinese.

1）The VTS guidelines require that the VTS authority should be provided with sufficient staff, appropriately qualified, suitably trained and capable of performing the tasks required, taking into consideration the type and level of services to be provided in conformity with the current IMO guidelines on the subject.

2）The Vessel Traffic Service is a service implemented by a competent authority, designed to improve the safety and efficiency of vessel traffic and protect the environment. The service should have the capability to interact with the traffic and to respond to traffic situations developing in the VTS area.

3）The International Convention on Maritime Search and Rescue was created in Hamburg, Germany on the 27th of April, 1979, so it is short for SAR. The important contents include the Organisation, cooperation, preparatory measures, operating procedures, and ship reporting system.

4）The basic concept of the GMDSS is the SAR ashore as well as shipping in the immediate vicinity of the ship in distress to be alerted, so they can participate in the coordinated SAR operation with the minimum delay.

5）The International Salvage Union is the trusted and unified global voice of its members who facilitate world trade by providing marine services which save lives, protect the environment, mitigate risk and reduce loss. The Union encourages high standards of operation and is conducted by its members.

Chapter Seven
Culture for Shipping Rules, Laws, Conventions

第七章
航运法规文化

本章学习目的及本章内容提要

　　航运法规是一个非常严谨的体系，有着自己的学科及专业特点，在航海类院校均设有海商法学科对航运法规进行系统地学习。本章的目的是让非海商法专业的学生了解航运法规的框架、了解航运法规形成的文化和内涵。本章主要包括国际海事公约介绍和中国海事法规介绍。

Lesson 19   Introductions to International
Maritime Conventions
第 19 课   国际海事公约介绍

There are several words regarding meanings of rules. For instance, rule, code, convention, practice, law, guideline, etc. Those may regulate the operations or practice for maritime purposes.

I . Introductions to the Framework of the International Maritime Conventions

There are a package of international maritime conventions defined by the IMO. The SOLAS, the MARPOL 73/78, and the STCW are the three pillars. In addition, the COLREG 72, the FAL 1965, the LL 66, the SAR 1979, the CSC 1972 are essential. Some conventions are made with other organisations. The significant international maritime conventions solely made by the IMO are listed in Table 19.1.

Table 19.1   List of Important International Maritime Conventions

No.	Name of the Important International Maritime Conventions
1	International Convention for the Safety of Life at Sea (SOLAS, 1974), as amended
2	International Convention for the Prevention of Pollution from Ships, 1973, as modified by the Protocol of 1978 relating thereto and by the Protocol of 1997 (MARPOL)
3	International Convention on Standards of Training, Certification and Watchkeeping for Seafarers (STCW) as amended, including the 1995 and 2010 Manila Amendments
4	Convention on the International Regulations for Preventing Collisions at Sea (COLREG), 1972
5	Convention on Facilitation of International Maritime Traffic (FAL), 1965
6	International Convention on Load Lines (LL), 1966
7	International Convention on Maritime Search and Rescue (SAR), 1979
8	Convention for the Suppression of Unlawful Acts Against the Safety of Maritime Navigation (SUA), 1988, and Protocol for the Suppression of Unlawful Acts Against the Safety of Fixed Platforms Located on the Continental Shelf (and the 2005 Protocols)
9	International Convention for Safe Containers (CSC), 1972
10	Convention on the International Maritime Satellite Organization (IMSO C), 1976

Continued

No.	Name of the Important International Maritime Conventions
11	The Torremolinos International Convention for the Safety of Fishing Vessels (SFV), 1977, superseded by The 1993 Torremolinos Protocol; Cape Town Agreement of 2012 on the Implementation of the Provisions of the 1993 Protocol relating to the Torremolinos International Convention for the Safety of Fishing Vessels
12	International Convention on Standards of Training, Certification and Watchkeeping for Fishing Vessel Personnel (STCW-F), 1995
13	Special Trade Passenger Ships Agreement (STP), 1971 and Protocol on Space Requirements for Special Trade Passenger Ships, 1973
14	International Convention Relating to Intervention on the High Seas in Cases of Oil Pollution Casualties (INTERVENTION), 1969
15	Convention on the Prevention of Marine Pollution by Dumping of Wastes and Other Matter (LC), 1972 (and the 1996 London Protocol)
16	International Convention on Oil Pollution Preparedness, Response and Co-operation (OPRC), 1990
17	Protocol on Preparedness, Response and Co-operation to Pollution Incidents by Hazardous and Noxious Substances, 2000 (OPRC-HNS Protocol)
18	International Convention on the Control of Harmful Anti-fouling Systems on Ships (AFS), 2001
19	International Convention for the Control and Management of Ships' Ballast Water and Sediments, 2004
20	The Hong Kong International Convention for the Safe and Environmentally Sound Recycling of Ships, 2009
21	International Convention on Civil Liability for Oil Pollution Damage (CLC), 1969
22	1992 Protocol to the International Convention on the Establishment of an International Fund for Compensation for Oil Pollution Damage (FUND 1992)
23	Convention relating to Civil Liability in the Field of Maritime Carriage of Nuclear Material (NUCLEAR), 1971
24	Athens Convention Relating to the Carriage of Passengers and Their Luggage by Sea (PAL), 1974
25	Convention on Limitation of Liability for Maritime Claims (LLMC), 1976
26	International Convention on Liability and Compensation for Damage in Connection with the Carriage of Hazardous and Noxious Substances by Sea (HNS), 1996 (and its 2010 Protocol)
27	International Convention on Civil Liability for Bunker Oil Pollution Damage, 2001
28	Nairobi International Convention on the Removal of Wrecks, 2007
29	International Convention on Tonnage Measurement of Ships (TONNAGE), 1969
30	International Convention on Salvage (SALVAGE), 1989
31	Convention on the International Maritime Organization

In addition to those conventions aforementioned, a few conventions or rules are made by the cooperation between the IMO and other organisations. The Maritime Labour Convention (2006) are made by the IMO and the ILO. International Aeronautical and Maritime Search and Rescue Manual are the operation manual made by the IMO and the International Civil Aviation Organisation (ICAO). Some laws or conventions are merely made by the other organisations. For example, the United Nations on the Law of the Sea (UNCLOS) is made by the United Nations.

II. Introductions to the SOLAS Convention

The SOLAS stands for the International Convention for the Safety of Life at Sea. The first version of the treaty was passed in 1914 in response to the sinking of the Royal Mailing Ship (RMS) *Titanic* attached to White Star Company. It prescribed numbers of lifeboats and other emergency equipment along with safety procedures, including continuous radio watches. The UK recommended a joint research on the creating of a convention called safety of life at sea. The IMCO was established in 1959 and the safety of life at sea had become an international convention and the name was changed into "the International Convention for the Safety of Life at Sea" (SOLAS).

Nowadays, there are two sections in SOLAS. Section A is the compulsory rules and Section B is the recommended rules. There are 14 chapters in both Section A and Section B. The 14 chapters are Chapter I—General Provisions, Chapter II—1—Construction-Subdivision and stability, machinery and electrical installations, Chapter II—2—Fire protection as well as fire detection and fire extinction, Chapter III—Life-saving appliances and arrangements, Chapter IV—Radiocommunications, Chapter V—Safety of navigation, Chapter VI—Carriage of cargoes and oil fuels, Chapter VII—Carriage of dangerous goods, Chapter VIII—Nuclear ships, Chapter IX—Management for the Safe Operation of Ships, Chapter X—Safety measures for high—speed craft, Chapter XI—1—Special measures to enhance maritime safety, Chapter XI—2—Special measures to enhance maritime security, Chapter XII—Additional safety measures for bulk carriers, Chapter XIII—Verification of compliance, Chapter XIV—Safety measures for ships operating in polar waters.

III. Introductions to STCW Convention

The STCW stands for the International Convention on Standard of Training, Certification, and Watchkeeping for Seafarers, 1978. It was the first international convention concerning competencies of seafarers. It was adopted during 14th of June and 7th of July, 1978. It was implemented at 28th of April of 1984. As early as 1960, the assembly of the SOLAS adopted a resolution on enhancement of education and training for seafarers. Intergovernmental Maritime Consultative Organization or the IMCO (renamed IMO after 22nd of May, 1982) and the ILO appealed for co-ordinations amongst all flag states administrations. There are several main causes to form the STCW. Firstly, the marine incidents, accidents, disasters have been increasing dramatically. Secondly, more Shipowners have been paying more attention to their businesses rather than safety of lives and property, qualifications and educations for seafarers vary from country to country. For example, there are four years academic educations on seafarers in China whereas there are a few months training programs in the Philippines. The definitions of seafarers' duties used to be much different. For example, the Chief Officer took charge of safety but the Second Officer took charge of cargo work in the Soviet Union. However, the Chief Officer took charge of cargo work and the Second Officer took charge of nautical charts, and publications as well as navaids in the western nations. For example, east European crewmembers might not work effectively on board west European ships. This is because they learnt in the Soviet Union system. After the termination of the cold war, the world needs a standard system to regulate the quality, education, and responsibility of the seafarer. There are international crew pools for works on board the same ships to form multinational crew ships, but the knowledge and skills are much different. Shipowners in the developed countries needed more seafarers from the developing countries. Therefore the international standards were required to be made. This is the background of the STCW.

Content Introduction. It includes Articles and Regulations. There are two parts, namely Section A—Compulsory rules and Section B—Recommended rules. There are 8 chapters in both Section A and Section B, including Chapter I—General Provisions, Chapter II—Master and Deck Department, Chapter III—Engine Department, Chapter IV—Radiocommunication and Radio Operators, Chapter V— Special Training Requirements for Personnel on Certain Types of Ships, Chapter VI—Emergency, Occupational Safety, Security, Medical Care and Survival Functions, Chapter VII—Alternative Certification, and Chapter VIII—Watchkeeping.

IV. Introductions to MARPOL 73/78

The MARPOL 73/78 stands for the Protocol of 1978 to the International Convention for the Prevention of Pollution from Ships, 1973. It was adopted by the International Conference on Marine Pollution concerned by the IMO from 8th October to 2nd November, 1973. Protocol (Provisions concerning Reports on Incidents involving Harmful Substances) and Protocol II (Arbitration) were adopted at the same Conference. This Convention was subsequently modified by the Protocol of 1978, relating thereto, which was adopted by the International Conference on Tanker Safety and Pollution Prevention (ISPP Conference) convened by the IMO from 6th to 17th February, 1978.

There are six annexes in MARPOL 73/78, including Annex I—Regulations for the Prevention of Pollution by Oil, Annex II—Regulations for the Control of Pollution by Noxious Liquid Substances in Bulk, Annex III—Regulations for the Prevention of Pollution by Harmful Substances Carried by Sea in Packaged Form, Annex IV—Regulations for the Prevention of Pollution by Sewage from Ships, Annex V—Regulations for the Prevention of

Pollution by Garbage from Ships, and Annex VI—Regulations for the Prevention of Air Pollution from Ships.

V. Other International Maritime Conventions

In addition to the three pillar maritime conventions, other conventions are also essential. The Search and Rescue Convention was adopted in Hamburg between April 9th and 27th, 1979. There are five chapters, including Chapter One—Terms and Definitions, Chapter Two—Organization and Coordination, Chapter Three Co—operation Between States, Chapter Four—Operating Procedures, Ship Reporting System.

The ICLL stands for the International Convention on Load Line. It was adopted by the IMCO between March 3rd and April 5th, 1966. There are 34 articles in the convention. The articles include Article 1—General Obligation under the Convention, Article 2—Definitions, Article 3—General Provisions, Article 4—Application, Article 5—Exceptions, Article 6—Exemptions, Article 7—Force Majeure, Article 8—Equvialents, Article 9—Approvals for Experimental Purposes, Article 10—Repairs, Alternations and Modifications, Article 11—Zones and Areas, Article 12—Submersion, Article 13—Survey, Inspection and Marking, Article 14—Initial and Periodical Surveys and Inspections, Article 15—Maintenance of Conditions after Survey, Article 16—Issue of Certificate, Article 17—Issue of Certificate by Another Government, Article 18—Form of Certificate, Article 19—Duration of Certificate, Article 20—Acceptance of Certificates, Article 21—Control, Article 22—Privileges, Article 23—Casualties, Article 24—Prior Treaties and Conventions, Article 25—Special Rules Drawn up by Agreement, Article 26—Communication of Information, Article 27—Signature, Acceptance, and Accession, Article 28—Coming into Force, Article 29—Amendments, Article 30—Denunciation, Article 31—Suspension, Article 32—Territories, Article 33—Registration, and Article 34—Languages.

The Tonnage 69 refers to the International Convention on Tonnage Measurement of Ships, 1969. It was adopted by the IMCO between May 27th and June 23rd, 1969. There are 22 articles in the convention. The articles include Article 1—General Obligation under the Convention, Article 2—Definitions, Article 3—Application, Article 4—Exeptions, Article 5—Force Majeure, Article 6—Determination of Tonnage, Article 7—Issue of Certificate, Article 8—Issue of Certificate by Another Government, Article 9—Form of Certificate, Article 10—Cancellation of Certificate, Article 11—Acceptance of Certificate, Article 12—Inspection, Article 13—Privileges, Article 14—Prior Treaties, Conventions, Arrangement, Article 15—Communication of Information, Article 16—Signature, Acceptance, and Accession, Article 17—Coming into Force, Article 18—Amendments, Article 19—Denuncation, Article 20—Territories, Article 21—Deposit and Registration, and Article 22—Languages.

The COLREG 72 stands for the International Regulations for Preventing Collision at Sea, 1972. It was made in 1972 and it was effective in 1977. It concerns traffic rules at sea.

There are five chapters in COLREG 72, including Chapter One—General, Chapter Two—Steering and Sailing Rules, Chapter Three—Lights and Shapes, Chapter Four—Sound and Light Signals, Chapter Five—Exemptions.

The Maritime Labour Convention was adopted by the International Labour Organization in February 2006. It is the cooperation convention between the ILO and the IMO. It was said that it was the fourth significant international maritime conventions after the three pillars. The 16 articles include Article 1—General Obligations, Article 2—Definitions and Scope of Application, Article 3—Fundamental Rights and Principles, Article 4—Seafarers' Employment and Social Rights, Article 5—Implementation and Enforcement Responsibilities, Article 6—Regulations and Parts A and B of the Code, Article 7—Consultation with Shipowners' and Seafarers' Organization, Article 8—Entry into Force, Article 9—Eenunciation, Article 10—Effect of Entry into Force, Article 11 and Article 12—Depository Functions, Article 13 and Article 14—Special Tripartite Committee, Article 14—Amendment of this Convention, Article 15—Amendments to the Code, Article 16—Authoritative Languages.

The UNCLOS stands for the United Nations Convention on the Law of the Sea. It was adopted in the United States in 1982. The convention mainly concerns inland waters, territorial seas, contiguous zone, exclusive economic zone, and high seas. It is used to consult the disputes of marine territory. There are 17 parts in the UNCLOS. The parts include Part 1—Use of Terms and Scopes, Part 2—Territorial Sea and Contiguous Zone, Part 3—Straits Used for International Navigation, Part 4—Archipelagic States, Part 5—Exclusive Economic Zone, Part 6—Continental Shelf, Part 7—High Seas, Part 8—Regime of Islands, Part 9—Enclosed or Semi-enclosed Seas, Part 10—Right of Access of Land—Locked States to and from the Sea and Freedom of Transit, Part 11—The Area, Part 12—Limitation on Jurisdiction of the Marine Environment, Part 13—Marine Scientific Research, Part 14—Development and Transfer of Marine Technology, Part 15—Settlement of Disputes, Part 16—General Provisions, and Part 17—Final Provisions

VI. Related Culture Words and Technical Terms

R.M.S *Titanic* (英国皇家邮轮"泰坦尼克号")—It was the largest cruise ship owned by White Star Company. At 1140 hours local time, 14th of April, 1912, R. M. S *Titanic* collided with an iceberg. At 0220 hours, 15th of April, 1912, she was sinking in position 41 degrees 43.5 minutes North, 49 degrees 56.8 minutes West. 1,502 crewmembers and passengers died. *Titanic* struck an iceberg and 4 compartments were flooding. The design of the ship is the maximum three compartments can be flooded without sinking. SOLAS convention was created because of the sinking of *Titanic*.

women and children first (妇女和儿童优先)—It is the rule created by Captain Edward Smith, the Captain of *Titanic*. That is to say, weaknesses will go first in the disaster. For example, we use the following sequence to evacuate from the abandoning vessel, injured person, women and children, passengers, crewmembers. The Shipmaster is the last person to evacuate from the abandoning vessel.

Amoco Cadiz disaster (阿莫科·加的斯)—It is a ship caused severe oil pollution in the English Channel. It contained 1,604,500 barrels (219,797 tons) of light crude oil from Ras Tanura, Saudi Arabia and Kharg Island, Iran. Severe weather resulting in the complete breakup of the ship before any oil could be pumped out of the wreck, resulting in its entire cargo of crude oil (belonging to Shell) and 4,000 tons of fuel oil being spilled into the sea.

go all out(全力以赴)—In general, it is used to say that other persons will provide assistance for persons or units in distress.

lessons to be learned (吸取教训)—In general, marine accidents are mothers of the international maritime conventions. All important conventions are from the severe accident.

VII. Exercises

1. Discuss with your classmates and answer the following questions.

1) What does the SOLAS stand for?

2) What does the MARPOL 73/78 stand for?

3) What does the STCW stand for?

4) Tell us the content of the SOLAS convention.

5) Tell us the annexes of the MARPOL 73/78.

6) Tell us the content of the STCW convention.

7) What does the ICLL 66 stand for?

8) What does the tonnage 69 stand for?

9) What does the UNCLOS stand for?

10) What does the COLREG 72 stand for?

2. Deep thinking.

1) Make differences among law, code, rule, convention, regulation, guidance.

2) What are three pillars of the international maritime conventions defined by the IMO?

3) Tell us the story of sinking of R.M.S *Titanic*.

4) Why do the IMO and the ILO start cooperation on the MLC 06?

5) List the content of the SOLAS convention. Why does it play significant role in maritime safety?

6) List the content of the STCW convention. Why is it important in international seafarers' market?

7) List the annexes of the MARPOL 73/78. Why do we mention 1973 and 1978 at the same time?

8) Are there any similarities between traffic rules at sea and traffic rules on land?

9) How important are the International Maritime Conventions?

10) How will you translate "前事不忘,后事之师"? Why do we connect it with the International Maritime Conventions?

3. Translate the following sentences into English.

1）《国际海上人命安全公约》是所有的涉及海事安全工作中最重要的公约,该公约的制定动因是英国白星公司的豪华邮轮"泰坦尼克"号沉没。

2）联合国海洋法公约早在 1982 年就已经签署,是各国之间解决领土争端的协调公约,其中 12 海里的海疆领土定义主要来自该公约。

3）《海员培训、发证和值班标准国际公约》能够协调船员适任标准。我国作为船员大国,我国的船员受到欧盟等国家的一致好评。我国船员输出已经和国际航运市场接轨。

4）人类对吨位丈量的认知可以追溯至 13 世纪,当时古人用拉斯特、酒桶、摩逊丈量法。比如拉斯特,一个拉斯特约等于 1 814.37 千克。

5）我国三国时期有"曹冲称象"的典故,这是人类对于船舶载重换算意识的萌芽。直到 1835 年西方才有劳埃德船级社发明了船舶载重计算方式。

4. Translate the following sentences into Chinese.

1）There are two parts in the MLC. Part A is mandatory and Part B is recommended. The contents include living conditions on board, food nutrition standards, working and rest hours, conditions of employment, sanitary conditions, leave pay, health conditions, etc.

2）The Plimsoll line, also called the Plimsoll mark, the official name for the International Load Line, is an internationally agreed-upon reference line marking the loading limit for cargo ships. At the instigation of one of its members, Samuel Plimsoll, a merchant and shipping reformer, the British Parliament, in the Merchant Shipping Act of 1875, provided for the marking of a load line on the hull of every cargo ship, indicating the maximum depth to which the ship could be safely loaded.

3）The COLREG 72 stands for the international regulations for preventing collision at sea, 1972. The rules regulate traffic rules at sea. In addition, the rules also regulate different types of lights and shapes used in different situations, the collision avoidance rules in different cases, and rules in restricted visibilities.

4）The IMDG stands for the International Maritime Dangerous Goods Code. The IMO published it in order to standardize the carriage of dangerous goods at sea. Nowadays, the majorities of marine cargoes are harmful materials to the marine environment. It is necessary to regulate the standards for the carriage of dangerous goods.

5）The IMO—the International Maritime Organization—is the United Nations specialized agency with responsibility for the safety and security of shipping and the prevention of marine and atmospheric pollution by ships. The IMO's work supports the UN sustainable development goals.

Lesson 20   Introductions to China Maritime Laws
第 20 课　　中国海事法规介绍

China is a country with very long coastlines, large amount of seawaters. It is therefore that the maritime laws are significant in China. The maritime laws are from the 1980s.

I . Constitutions of Maritime Courts in China

In November of 1984 the maritime courts were established under "decision on establishment of maritime courts in coastal cities" of the People's Congress of China and "decision on setting up maritime courts" of Supreme People's Court decided to set up Maritime Courts. In Shanghai, Tianjin, Guangzhou, Qingdao, Dalian, and Wuhan, Maritime Courts were established thereafter. By 2019, there will be 11 Maritime Courts in China. In addition to the maritime courts aforementioned Beihai Maritime Court, Nanjing Maritime Court, and Haikou Maritime Court are also founded.

II . Introductions to Constitution of Maritime Law in China

In general, there are several stages for the implementation of maritime laws. The laws will be submitted to the National People's Congress of the People's Republic of China. The Standing Committee of the National People's Congress will hold a session on study of the maritime laws. While the maritime law has been permitted after consultation, the President of the People's Republic of China will sign the document in the Order of the President of the People's Republic of China. Then the maritime law will be entered into force as the time set in the law.

Maritime Administration Rules shall be approved by the State Council of the People's Republic of China and signed by the Primer of the People's Republic of China. For example, Regulations of the People's Republic of China Concerning the Administration of Traffic Safety on Inland Waters is the rule approved by Primer of the People's Republic of China. Hence it is not the maritime law and it is the maritime rule instead.

Maritime Administration Order is another type of maritime rules. Maritime Orders will be signed and approved by the Minister of the Ministry of Transport. For instance, China Security Code for International Ships and Rules of Administration Procedures for Transport of China are maritime administration orders.

III. Laws for Mother Rivers

1. **Yellow River Protection Law of the People's Republic of China** was adopted at the 37th Meeting of the Standing Committee of the Thirteenth National People's Congress on October 30, 2022. It was signed in the Order No. 123 of the President of the People's Republic of China on October 30, 2022. The main content includes Chapter Ⅰ—General Provisions, Chapter Ⅱ—Planning and Control, Chapter Ⅲ—Ecological Protection and Restoration, Chapter Ⅳ Conservation and Intensive Utilization of Water Resources, Chapter Ⅴ—Water and Sediment Control and Flood Control Safety, Chapter Ⅵ—Pollution Prevention and Control, Chapter Ⅶ Promoting High—Quality Development, Chapter Ⅷ Protection, Inheritance, and Promotion of the Yellow River Culture, Chapter Ⅸ Guarantee and Supervision, Chapter Ⅹ Legal Liability, and Chapter Ⅺ Supplemental Provisions.

2. **The Yangtze River Protection Law of the People's Republic of China** was adopted at the 24th Meeting of the Standing Committee of the Thirteenth National People's Congress on December 26, 2020. It was signed in the Order No. 65 of the President of the People's Republic of China on December 26, 2020. The main content includes Chapter Ⅰ—General Provisions, Chapter Ⅱ—Plan and Control, Chapter Ⅲ—Resource Protection, Chapter Ⅳ—Prevention and Control of Water Pollution, Chapter Ⅴ—Ecological Protection and Environment Remediation, Chapter Ⅵ—Green Development, Chapter Ⅶ—Guarantee and Supervision, Chapter Ⅷ—Legal Liability, Chapter Ⅸ—Supplementary Provisions. It was approved by the Order No. 65 of the President of the People's Republic of China on December 26th, 2020.

IV. Maritime Laws

1. **Maritime Traffic Safety Law of the People's Republic of China** was adopted at the 2nd Meeting of the Standing Committee of the Sixth National People's Congress on September 2, 1983; amended according to the Decision on Amending the Foreign Trade Law of the People's Republic of China and Other Eleven Laws at the 24th Meeting of the Standing Committee of the 12th National People's Congress on November 7, 2016; revised at the 28th Meeting of the Standing Committee of the 13th National People's Congress on April 29th, 2021. The latest version was signed in the Order No. 79 of the President of the People's Republic of China on April 29, 2021. The main content includes Chapter Ⅰ—General Provisions, Chapter Ⅱ—Vessels, Offshore Facilities, Crewmembers, Chapter Ⅲ—Maritime Traffic Conditions and Navigation Guarantee, Chapter Ⅳ—Navigation, Berthing, and Operation, Chapter Ⅴ—Safety of Maritime Passenger and Freight Transportation, Chapter Ⅵ—Maritime Search and Rescue, Chapter Ⅶ—Investigation and Handling of Maritime Traffic Accident, Chapter Ⅷ—Supervision and Administration, Chapter Ⅸ—Legal Liabilities, and Chapter Ⅹ—Supplemental Provisions.

2. **Marine Environmental Protection Law of the People's Republic of China** was adopted

at the 24th Meeting of the Standing Committee of the 5th National People's Congress on August 23, 1982 at the first time. The law was amended several times. The latest three amendments are as follows: The first amendment version was adopted at the 24th Meeting of the Standing Committee of the 12th National People's Congress on November 7, 2016. The second amendment version was adopted at the 30th Meeting of the Standing Committee of the 12th National People's Congress on November 4, 2017. The third amendment version was adopted at the 6th Meeting of the Standing Committee of the 14th National People's Congress on October 24, 2023. The latest version was signed in Order No. 12 of the President of the People's Republic of China on October 23, 2023.

The main content includes Chapter I—General Provisions, Chapter II—Prevention of Pollution Damage to the Marine Environment by Coastal Construction Projects, Chapter III—Prevention of Pollution Damage to the Marine Environment by Offshore Oil Exploration and Exploitation, Chapter IV—Prevention of Pollution Damage to the Marine Environment by Land—sourced Pollutant, Chapter V—Prevention of Pollution Damage to the Marine Environment by Vessels, Chapter VI—Prevention of Pollution Damage to the Marine Environment by Dumping of Wastes, Chapter VII—Legal Liabilities, and Chapter VIII—Supplementary Provisions.

3. **Law of the People's Republic of China on Prevention and Control of Water Pollution** was adopted at the 5th Meeting of the Standing Committee of the 6th National People's Congress on May 11, 1984 for the first time. The first amendment version was adopted at the 19th Meeting of the Standing Committee of the 8th National People's Congress on May 15, 1996. The second amendment version was adopted at the 28th Meeting of the Standing Committee of the 12th National People's Congress on June 27, 2017. The latest version was signed in Order No.70 of the President of the People's Republic of China on June 27, 2017. There are 8 chapters in the Law, namely Chapter I—General Provisions, Chapter II—Standards and Planning for Water Pollution Prevention and Control, Chapter III—Supervision and Administration for Water Pollution Prevention and Control, Chapter IV—Measures for Water Pollution Prevention and Control, Chapter V—Protection of Drinking Water Sources and Other Special Waters, Chapter VI—Management of Water Pollution Accidents, Chapter VII—Legal Liability, and Chapter VIII—Supplementary Provisions.

4. **Coast Guard Law of the People's Republic of China** was adopted at the 25th Meeting of the Standing Committee of the 13th National People's Congress on January 22, 2021 for the first time. It was signed in the Order No. 71 of the President of the People's Republic of China on January 22, 2021. There are 11 chapters in the law, including Chapter I—General Provisions, Chapter II—Agencies and Duties, Chapter III—Maritime Security, Chapter IV—Maritime Administrative Law Enforcement, Chapter V—Investigation of Maritime Crimes, Chapter VI—Use of Police Equipment and Weapons, Chapter VII—Guarantees and Cooperation, Chapter VIII—International Cooperation, Chapter IX—Supervision, Chapter X—Legal Liability, and Chapter XI—Supplemental Provisions.

5. **Port Law of the People's Republic of China** was adopted at the 3rd Meeting of the Standing Committee of the 10th National People's Congress on June 28, 2003 at the first time. The first amendment version was adopted at the 14th Meeting of the Standing Committee of the 12th National People's Congress on April 24, 2015. The second amendment version was adopted at the 30th Meeting of the Standing Committee of the 12th National People's Congress on November 4, 2017. The third amendment version was adopted at the 7th Meeting of the Standing Committee of the 13th National People's Congress on December 29, 2018. The latest version was signed in Order No.23 of the President of the People's Republic of China on December 29, 2018. There are 6 chapters in the law, including Chapter Ⅰ—General Provisions, Chapter Ⅱ—Port Planning and Construction, Chapter Ⅲ—Business Operation of Ports, Chapter Ⅳ—Port Safety and Supervision, Chapter Ⅴ—Legal Liabilities, and Chapter Ⅵ—Supplementary Provisions.

6. **Waterway Law of the People's Republic of China** was adopted at the 12th Meeting of the Standing Committee of the 12th National People's Congress on December 28, 2014. It was signed in Order No.17 of the President of the People's Republic of China on December 28, 2014. There are 7 chapters in the law, namely Chapter Ⅰ—General Provisions, Chapter Ⅱ—Fairway Planning, Chapter Ⅲ—Fairway Construction, Chapter Ⅳ—Fairway Maintenance, Chapter Ⅵ—Legal Liability, and Chapter Ⅶ—Supplementary Provisions.

7. **Maritime Law of the People's Republic of China** was first adopted at the 28th Meeting of the Standing Committee of the 7th National People's Congress on November 7th, 1992. It was signed in Order No.64 of the President of the People's Republic of China on November 7, 1992. There are 15 Chapters in the law. Chapter I involves General Provisions. Chapter II concerns Ships. It includes Section 1—Ownership of Ships, Section 2—Mortgage of Ships, and Section 3—Maritime Liens. Chapter III talks about Crew. it includes Section 1—Basic Principles and Section 2—The Master. Chapter Ⅳ deals with Chapter Ⅳ—Contract of Carriage Goods by Sea. It includes Section 1—Basic Principles, Section 2—Carrier's Responsibilities, Section 3— Shipper's Responsibilities, Section 4—Transport Documents, Section 5—Delivery of Goods, Section 6—Cancellation of Contract, Section 7—Special Provisions Regarding Voyage Charter Party, and Section 8—Special Provisions Regarding Multimodal Transport Contract. Chapter V is Contract of Carriage of Passengers by Sea. Chapter VI concerns Charter Parties. It includes Section 1—Basic Principles, Section 2—Time Charter Party, and Section 3—Bareboat Charter Party. Chapter Ⅶ concerns Contract of Sea Towage, and Chapter Ⅷ deals with Collision of Ships. Chapter Ⅸ—Salvage at Sea tells Chapter Ⅹ—General Average and Chapter Ⅺ deals with Limitation of Liability for Maritime Claims. Chapter Ⅻ focuses on Contract of Marine Insurance. It includes Section 1—Basic Principles, Section 2—Conclusion, Termination and Assignment of Contract, Section 3—Obligations of the Insured, Section 4—Liability of the Insurer, Section 5—Loss of Damage to Subject Matter Insured and Abandonment, and Section 6—Payment of Indemnity. Chapter ⅩⅢ deals with Limitation of Time and Chapter ⅩⅣ concerns Application of Law Relation to

Foreign Related Matters. Chapter XV is Supplementary Provisions.

8. **Fisheries Law of the People's Republic of China** was adopted at the 14th Meeting of the Standing Committee of the 6th National People's Congress on January 20, 1986. The first amendment version was adopted at the 18th Meeting of the Standing Committee of the 9th National People's Congress on October 31, 2000. The second amendment version was adopted at the 11th Meeting of the Standing Committee of the 10th National People's Congress on August 28, 2004. The latest amendment version was signed in Order No.25 of the President of the People's Republic of China on August 28, 2004. There are 6 chapters in the law, including Chapter I —General Provisions, Chapter II—Aquaculture, Chapter III—Fishing, Chapter IV—Increase and Protection of Fishery Resources, Chapter V—Legal Liabilities, and Chapter VI—Supplementary Provisions

9. **Special Maritime Procedure Law of the People's Republic of China** was adopted at the 13th Meeting of the Standing Committee of the 9th National People's Congress on December 25, 1999. It was signed in Order No.28 of the President of the People's Republic of China on December 25, 1999. There are 12 chapters in the law. Chapter I is General Principles and Chapter II is Jurisdiction. The title of Chapter III is Preservation of Maritime Claims. It includes Section 1—General Provisions, Section 2—Arrest and Auction of Ships, and Section 3 Attachment and Auction of Cargo Carried by Ships. The title of Chapter IV is Maritime Injunction and the title of Chapter V is Preservation of Maritime Evidence. The title of Chapter VI is Maritime Security and the title of Chapter VII is Delivery. Chapter VIII focuses on Trial Procedure. The content includes Section 1—Provisions for Trial of Collision Cases, Section 2—Provisions for Trial of General Average Cases, Section 3—Provisions for Exercising the Right of Subrogation by Marine Insurers, and Section 4—Summary Procedure, Procedure for Exhortation and Procedure for Public. Chapter IX talks about Procedure for Constitution of Limitation Fund for Maritime Claims. The title of Chapter X is Procedure for Registration and Satisfaction of Claims while the title of Chapter XI is Procedure for Interpellation of Maritime Liens. Chapter XII deals with Supplementary Provisions

10. **Law of the People's Republic of China on the Administration of the Use of Sea Areas** was adopted at the 24th Meeting of the Standing Committee of the 9th National People's Congress on December 25, 1999. It was signed by President in Order No.61 of the President of the People's Republic of China on October 27, 2001. There are 8 chapters in the law.

Those include Chapter I —General Provisions, Chapter II —Marine Function Zoning, Chapter III—Application for, and Examination and Approval of the Use of Sea Areas, Chapter IV Right to the Use of Sea Areas, Chapter V—Fees for the Use of Sea Areas, Chapter VI—Supervision and Inspection, Chapter VII—Legal Liabilities, and Chapter VIII—Supplementary Provisions.

V. Related Culture Words and Technical Terms

running the country by law（依法治国）—It is a significant rule recommended by President Xi Jinping. Therefore maritime laws are still in building to meet the requirements.

Maritime Cases Dealing（海事案件处理）—In common practice, there are two layers for maritime cases, namely the maritime court, and the Higher People's Court. If a maritime case has been judged by the maritime court (Dalian Maritime Court), the case will be carried out. But one of the parties has the right to appeal to the Higher People's Court (Liaoning Higher People's Court) and the Higher People's Court's decision will be the final.

The International Cooperation Bureau of the Ministry of Transport of the People's Republic of China（中国交通运输部国际合作司）—It is a department in the MoT to deal with the international cooperation policies and related affairs. It is responsible for foreign affairs and is responsible for implementation of the international conventions, etc.

Policy and Legislation Division of China MSA（中国海事局政策法规处）—It is the department of China MSA of MoT of the People's Republic of China. The functions of the department should include but are not limited to: 1) organize to make policies, rules and codes concerning maritime issues; 2) organize to make standards for statutory surveys and inspections for fixtures at sea and ships; 3) manage legislation work in the national maritime fields and organize surveillance and inspection on the carrying out; 4) supervise national Administration Work and organizes the inspection.

VI. Exercises

1. Discuss with your classmates and answer the following questions.

1) How do we translate "中华人民共和国海商法" into English?

2) How do we translate "中华人民共和国海洋环境保护法" into English?

3) How do we translate "中华人民共和国水污染防治法" into English?

4) How do we translate "中华人民共和国长江保护法" into English?

5) How do we translate "中华人民共和国港口法" into English?

6) How do we translate "中华人民共和国海警法" into English?

7) How do we translate "中华人民共和国海事诉讼特别程序法" into English?

8) How do we translate "中华人民共和国渔业法" into English?

9) How do we translate "中华人民共和国海上交通安全法" into English?

10) How do we translate "中华人民共和国内河交通安全管理条例" into English?

2. Deep thinking.

1) Where can you find out the official English translation for a particular maritime law in China?

2) Where can you find out the date of permit and date of implementation?

3) Why do we focus on website of the National People's Congress of the People's Republic of China?

4）What are the differences among maritime laws，maritime rules，and maritime administration orders in China?

5）What do the laws on maritime traffic routes concern?

6）Please tell us the main content of port laws in China.

7）Please tell us the main content of protection law on the Yellow Sea.

8）Please tell us the main content of protection law for the marine environment in China.

9）Please show us the construction on one particular law. For example the history of the amendments.

10）What are called fairways? Can you give us more words with similar meanings?

3. Translate the following sentences into English.

1）国务院渔业行政主管部门主管全国的渔业工作。县级以上地方人民政府渔业行政主管部门主管本行政区域内的渔业工作。县级以上人民政府渔业行政主管部门可以在重要渔业水域、渔港设渔政监督管理机构。

2）海上维权执法工作坚持中国共产党的领导，贯彻总体国家安全观，遵循依法管理、综合治理、规范高效、公正文明的原则。

3）港口总体规划，是指一个港口在一定时期的具体规划，包括港口的水域和陆域范围、港区划分、吞吐量和到港船型、港口的性质和功能、水域和陆域使用、港口设施建设岸线使用、建设用地配置以及分期建设序列等内容。

4）任何单位和个人都有保护海洋环境的义务，并有权对污染海洋环境、破坏海洋生态的单位和个人，以及海洋环境监督管理人员的违法行为进行监督和检举。

5）国务院自然资源主管部门会同国务院有关部门定期组织长江流域土地、矿产、水流、森林、草原、湿地等自然资源状况调查，建立资源基础数据库，开展资源环境承载能力评价，并向社会公布长江流域自然资源状况。

4. Translate the following sentences into Chinese.

1）The harbour superintendence agencies of the People's Republic of China shall be the competent authorities responsible for the unified supervision and administration of traffic safety in the coastal waters. Vessels and their major equipment relating to navigation safety must have valid technical certificates issued by vessel inspection departments.

2）The ownership of a ship means the shipowner's rights to lawfully possess, utilize, profit from and dispose of the ship in his ownership. With respect to a state-owned ship operated by an enterprise by the whole people having owned person status granted by the State, the provisions of this Code regarding the Shipowner shall apply to that legal person.

3）Measures must be taken to protect the aquatic resources when building harbours and oil terminals, as well as water conservancy facilities and tidal power stations in estuaries. Dams to be built across fish and crab migration routes shall be provided with appropriate fish passage facilities.

4）Water pollution refers to a change in the chemical, physical, biological or radioactive characteristics of water bodies due to the intervention of certain substances that affect the effective use of water, cause harm to people's health or damage the ecosystem and environment and results in a deterioration of water quality.

5）The port mentioned in the present law means an area composed of a certain scope of water area and land area, which has the functions for vessels to enter and exit, to berth, to anchor, for passengers to embark and disembark, and for goods to be loaded and unloaded, lightered, stored, etc., and which has the corresponding wharf facilities.

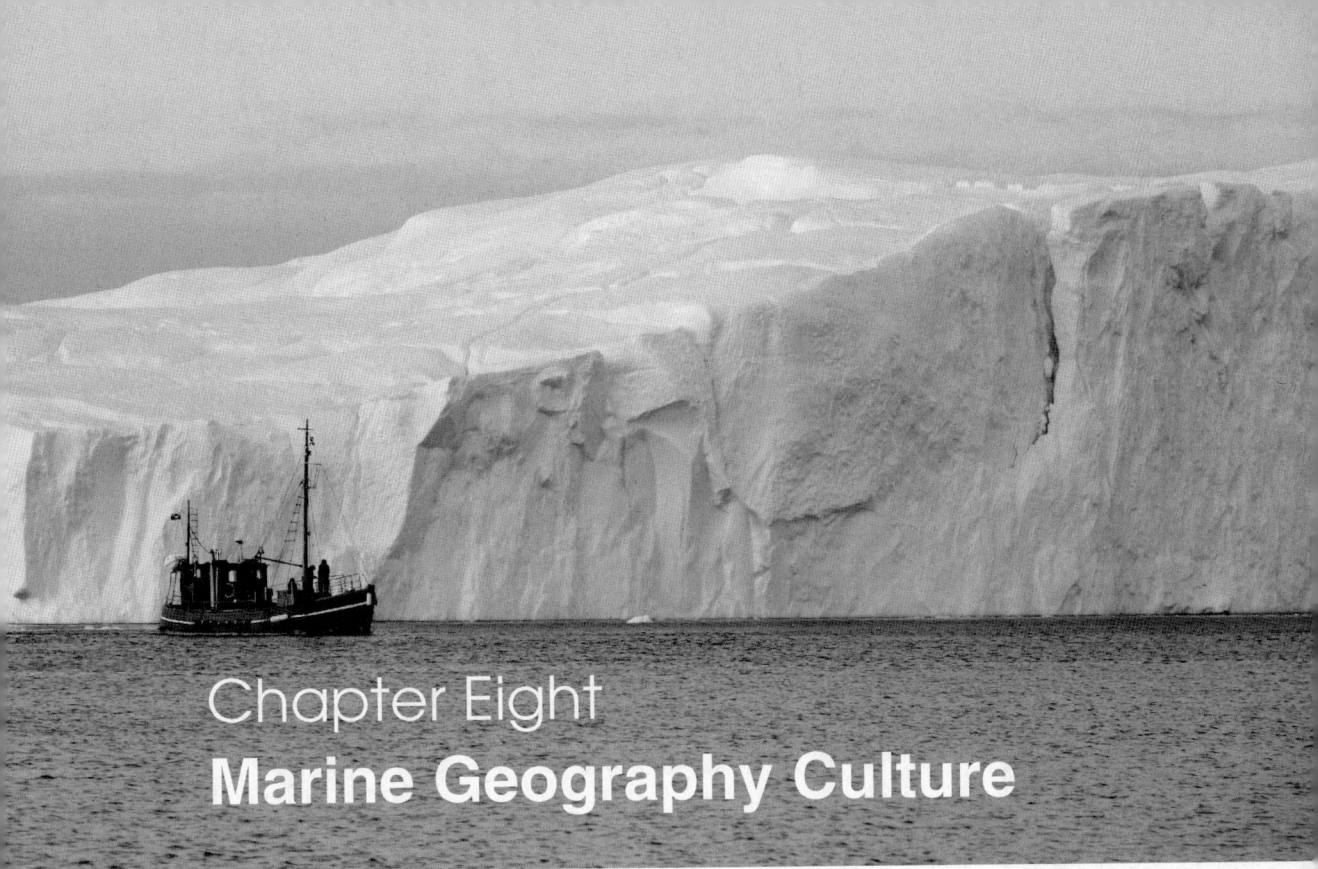

Chapter Eight
Marine Geography Culture

第八章
航运地理文化

本章学习目的及本章内容提要

本章的航运地理系指全球的大洋、内海、港湾、海峡、航线、运河及港口知识。同时还讲解了中国海运地理知识。通过本章学习让学生掌握这些航海地理文化，并热爱中国海洋疆土，自觉维护中国海洋疆土权益。

Lesson 21 Introductions to Oceans, Sea Routes, and Marine Waters of China
第 21 课 大洋、航路、国内海域介绍

In the vast earth, oceans account for 71%. There are four major on the earth. They are listed in the descending order, the Pacific Ocean, the Atlantic Ocean, the Indian Ocean, and the Arctic Ocean.

I. Introductions to Oceans

1. The Pacific Ocean

The Pacific Ocean Starts from the South Polar Areas to the North Pole, and starts westward from Asia and southward from Australia to the eastward North America and South America. It is the largest ocean in the world and it takes up one-third of the surface of the earth. Except for the sub-oceans or seas near the coast, it is approximately 179,679 square kilometres. It is twice that of the Atlantic Ocean. The average depth is 4,280 metres. The maximum depth is 11,034 metres. There are several sub-seas in the Pacific Ocean, such as Bering Sea, Sea of Ochotsk, Sea of Japan, Bohai, Huanghai (the Yellow Sea), East China Sea, South China Sea, Java Sea, etc. Major straits include Taiwan Haixia (Taiwan Strait), Bering Strait, Strait of Malacca and Korea Strait.

2. The Atlantic Ocean

It is the Second Largest Ocean in the World. It accounts for 20% of the earth's surface. It connects to Europe on the northeast, Africa on the southeast, North America on the northwest, South America on the southwest and Antarctica on the south. The further north started from Iceland (冰岛) to the further south Antarctica. The length of the North and South is 14,120 kilometres. The width of the equator is approximately 2,400 kilometres. The average depth is 3,597 metres. The maximum depth is 9,218 metres in Puerto Rico Trench. The area is 93,363 square kilometres. The North connects with the Indian Ocean with the Suez Canal. Sub-seas include the Mediterranean Sea, Caribbean Sea, North Sea, and Baltic Sea.

3. The Indian Ocean

The name was gotten because it is located in the south of the Indian Peninsula. In the ancient time , it was called Erythrea in Greek (484 BCE–425 BCE). It means the Red Sea. Now the Red Sea was shrunk to the place near Egypt. The area is 74,920 square kilometres and the average depth is 3,711 metres.

The west starts from East Africa. The north starts from South Asia. The south starts from Antarctica. The east starts from Strait of Malacca and Singapore.

There are more seas and gulfs than any other ocean. The seas and gulfs include Red Sea, Arabic Sea, Gulf of Aden, Persian Gulf, Gulf of Oman, Bay of Bengal, Andaman Sea, Arafura Sea, Timor Sea, Gulf of Carpentaria, Great Australian Bight, and Mozambique Channel.

4. The Arctic Ocean

It is only 14,750 square kilometres. It is 1/14 of the Pacific Ocean. It accounts for 4.1% of the world's Ocean. The average depth is 1,225 metres and the maximum depth is 5,527 metres. On the whole, it is not deep. It is surrounded by continents. It connects to the Atlantic Ocean with Norwegian Sea, Greenland Sea, and Baffin Bay. It connects to the Pacific Ocean with Bering Strait. The following countries or areas connect to the Arctic Ocean: Canada, Greenland (Denmark), Alaska (USA), Norway, Finland, Russia, and Sweden.

II. Introductions to Traffic Routes

There are thousands of ships sailing at sea. Ships normally sail at traditional routes. Suppose that we put China ports in the centre, we can see the routes pass through every corner of the world. Sea Routes are significant because they are important in passage plan-making and maritime logistics. In the Chinese concept, the sea routes are divided into long routes, middle routes, and short routes or coastal routes.

1. Long Range Sea Routes

Trans-Pacific Ocean Route. This route is one of the busiest routes in the world because the most significant economic bodies (China, Japan, and the USA) surround the ocean. The international business makes the transportation in this area very busy. In the Pacific Ocean, there are routes starting from China, the East ports of Russia, ROK, Japan, the Philippines, Malaysia, Singapore, and Indonesia and terminating at west ports of North America or South America. In addition, the transpacific ships may transit Panama Canal and arrive in ports in Caribbean countries, such as Cuba, Bahamas, Haiti, Dominican Republic, Jamaica, Puerto Rico, etc. Furthermore, there are routes starting from the Far East to Australia and New Zealand. There are also routes starting from Australia and New Zealand and terminating at ports in North America.

Trans-Atlantic Ocean Route. As Europe countries and USA surround the Ocean, that makes the routes busy. The north routes between West European Ports and ports on the East Coast of North America are the major routes. Some ships may transit Panama Canal and get alongside the ports on the West Coast of North America. Many large vessels depart from European ports and detour the entire African Continent and arrive in ports in South Asia.

Trans-Indian Ocean Route. The oil route is the cornerstone of the sea routes in the Indian Ocean. Since crude oil is to be transported from the Persian Gulf. For instance, oil tankers may go across half of the Indian Ocean and transit the Strait of Malacca and Singapore and pass through the South China Sea and East China Sea. Then the ships arrive in Shanghai ports and other northern ports in China.

2. Middle Routes

In the concept of Chinese Transport Field, the middle routes are shorter than trans-ocean routes. For instance, ships depart from ports in China and sailed downward to ports in Australia and New Zealand. For another example, ships departed from ports in China and sail eastward to ports in Japan or South East Asia. In addition, ships depart from ports of China and sail downward and transit the Strait of Malacca to South Asia or the Middle East.

3. Coastal Routes

In the concept of Chinese Transport Field, the coastal routes refer to the North-South Sea Routes. Though the Dalian-Fangcheng Sea Routes are longer than most of the Sino-Japan Sea Routes, they are treated as short sea routes. Most coastal routes are not far away from the land whatever the distance from the land.

III. Introductions to Canals

Canals are channel cut through land for boats or ships to travel along, or to carry water for irrigation. In other words, it is the artificial waterway or artificially improved river used for travel, shipping, or irrigation. Canals are different from rivers, streams, and natural waters, but they are made use of natural water systems, such as rivers, lakes, or others.

1. Dayunhe (Beijing and Hangzhou Grand Canal)—The Longest Canal in the World

Dayunhe (Beijing and Hangzhou Grand Canal) is the longest canal in the world. It was used to transport grains, salt and other important goods and the transportation is called Caoyun (漕运) in Chinese. The canal was also used as the mailing system. The original building started since 486 BCE, and it is the earliest canal in the world.

The Grand Canal starts from Beijing to Hangzhou. It goes across Beijing, Tianjin cities and Hebei, Shandong, Henan, Anhui, Jiangshu, and Zhejiang provinces. The total length is 1,797 kilometres. It connects five rivers including Haihe (in Tianjin), Yellow River, Huaihe, Changjiang (the Yangtze River), and Qiantangjiang (in Hangzhou). Ancient Chinese made use of the Grand Canal to achieve transportation, entertainment, and so forth. It was not only used for the economy, but also for the culture. Though it started since Chunqiu Dynasty (the Spring and Autumn Period), and the Warring States Period, the Canal was enlarged in different dynasties, such as the Qin Dynasty, the Han Dynasty, the Wei and the Jin Dynasties, and the Northern and Southern Dynasty. In Sui Dynasty, the building of the Canal was at the peak. In the Yuan Dynasty, the Canal was straightened. That becomes the main part of the Canal we see today. The important ports are, for example, Beijing, Tianjin, Xuzhou, Yangzhou, Suzhou, and Hangzhou.

In addition to Beijing and Hangzhou Grand Canal, Suez Canal, Panama Canal, and Kiel

Canal are nowadays three important international shipping canals in the world, as they are significant in ocean transportation in the world.

2. Suez Canal—Connection Between the Red Sea and the Mediterranean Sea

Suez Canal is the separation between Asia and Africa continents. It is located in Egypt. As the canal building started from Pharaoh Senusret Ⅲ and the canal was named at that period. It connects the Red Sea and the Mediterranean Sea. The ships may transit the Suez Canal and avoid the detour of African Continent. The total length of the canal is 173 kilometres including extending part to the Mediterranean Sea. The width of the canal varies from 60 to 100 metres. Ships with a maximum draft of 11.5 metres are able to transit the canal, so the canal has its own limitations. Ships with a minimum draft of 11. 5 metres have to detour Africa Continent instead. There are four lakes in the passage of the canal, namely Lake Manzala, Lake Timsah, Great Bitter Lake, and Little Bitter Lake. Hence the Suez Canal is an artificial river in terms of the water system in the isthmus and the purpose is used for shipping. Nowadays, it is one of the busiest canals in the world.

3. Panama Canal—Connections Between the Pacific Ocean and the Atlantic Ocean

Panama Canal, as the name suggests, is located in the Republic of Panama. It is one of the most important passages in the world. The canal is unique since locks are used to solve the insufficient depth of water. Panama Canal was used for shipping in 1914. The narrowest width of the canal is 152 metres. The total length of the canal is around 82 kilometres. Panama Canal was widened and it started for use on June 26, 2016. In 1534, Spanish surveyed Panama Isthmus under the order of Spanish King Charles Ⅴ and prepared for canal making. However, the canal excavation ceased due to independent war. Following the busy international transportation, the canal excavation plays an important role in order to shorten the voyages between the Atlantic and the Pacific Oceans. Not all ships are suitable to transit the Panama Canal. Ships with a maximum length of 289. 56 metres, and maximum width, 32.31 metres, and a maximum draft 11.3 metres are permitted to transit the canal.

4. Kiel Canal—Connections Between North Sea and Baltic Sea

Kiel Canal is located in Germany and it connects the North Sea and Baltic Sea. The total length is 98.26 kilometres. The mean depth of water is 11 metres. The widest place is 162 metres and the narrowest place is 102.5 metres. The canal was built in 1887. In 1895, the canal began for use. The canal was built largely during the periods of 1907 and 1914 as well as 1965 and 1990. Nowadays, it has become one of the busiest canals in the world.

Ⅳ. Important Straits

Terms of strait, channel, and passage are used to describe narrow places between two river banks, lands, or continents. It is a naturally formed, narrow, typically navigable waterway that connects two larger bodies of water. For example, Three Gorges in Changjiang (the Yangtze River) are narrow places for two banks. Bering Strait is the narrow channel for two continents.

1. Straits in the Pacific Oceans

Bering Strait is a strait in the Pacific Ocean, which separates Asia and America continent. It is also the separation between Russia and the USA. The Strait was named after Danish explorer Vitus Bering. The northwest part of the Strait is a cape which is located in the northeast part of Russia. The cape (in the name of Cape Dezhnyov or Cape Dezhnev) is located in the northeaster most point Chukchi Peninsula of Russia in the Asia Continent. The cape's name was after Semyon Dezhnev, the Russian navigator who explored it in 1648. The east part of Bering Strait is Cape Prince of Wales, the extreme west part of Alaska state United States. Nowadays, more and more ships are operating in the Arctic waters and it is envisaged that Bering Strait will become more important than before.

Strait of Malacca is the strait between Malay Peninsula and Sumatra Island of Indonesia. It is located in the west part of the Pacific Ocean and the east part of the Indian Ocean. In other words, it links the Indian Ocean with South China Sea. Malaysia, Singapore, and Indonesia are involved in Strait of Malacca. Singapore is at the southern end of the Strait. It is an important channel for international shipping.

Korea Strait is a strait which connects East China Sea and Sea of Japan. The Southwest end is East China Sea where as the northeast end is Sea of Japan.

Strait of Magellan is located in the extreme south of South America Continent and it is surrounded by Tierra del Fuego (火地岛) and other islands. The name was gotten by Portuguese navigator Ferdinand Magellan's first passage in 1520. It connects the south of the Atlantic Ocean with the south of the Pacific Ocean. It was one of the important routes around South America continent before the Panama Canal was in use.

Taiwan Haixia (Taiwan Strait) and Qiongzhou Haixia (Qiongzhou Strait) are two important straits in the south of China. Two channels are inland waters of the People's Republic of China. Since the mainland of China is located in the north coast while Hainan province and Taiwan province are located in the south coasts. Both straits are significant for ships operating in the north-south coastal shipping line of China, since the strong and prosperous shipping in China.

2. Straits in the Atlantic Ocean

The English Channel is the separation between the British Isles and European Continent. It looks like an arm of the Atlantic Ocean on the basis of the shape on the map. The name was gotten because of the UK is on the west coast of the strait. It is simply called the Channel in some cases. The name English Channel has been widely used since the early 18th century because it was in Dutch Sea map to use the name. In the north, it connects the North Sea, and it connects the Mediterranean Sea and the main body of the Atlantic Ocean in the south. The narrowest part is called Strait of Dover because of the southeast port of Dover of the United Kingdom.

Strait of Gibraltar is located between the south of Spain and northwest part of the African continent. It is a narrow strait that connects the Atlantic Ocean to the Mediterranean Sea and separates the Iberian Peninsula in Europe from Morocco in Africa. Its western limits are Cape Trafalgar (Spain) and Cape Spartel (Morocco); its eastern limits Gibraltar and Point Almina (just E of Ceuta, NW Africa). It is the separation between Africa and Europe. The name was from Gibraltar which is located in the south of Iberian Peninsula of European Continent.

Drake Passage is a strait between Cape Horn and the south of Sheland Islands. It connects the southern Atlantic Ocean and the Pacific Ocean. It is the separation between South American Continent and Antarctica Continent. The name was from British navigator Sir Francis who was the first Englishman to sail around the world.

3. Strait in the Indian Ocean

Mandab Strait (the Bab-el-Mandeb) is a strait between Yemen on the Arabian Peninsula, and Djibouti and Eritrea in the Horn of Africa. It connects the Red Sea to the Gulf of Aden. It is the connection between the Indian Ocean and the Mediterranean Sea at large. It is the door of the Suez Canal. The meaning of the name is the Gate of Tears which means wrecks were occasionally seen in the area and were dangerous for navigation in ancient times.

Strait of Hormuz is the strait between the Persian Gulf and the Gulf of Oman. Iran is located on the north whereas Oman and the United Arab Emirates are located on the south. It is the only sea passage for sailing ships operating in the Gulf. Meanwhile the Persian Gulf is significant for world oil transportation, so we use a metaphor to say the strait is the gate of the Gulf. The name was from Hormuz Island which is located in the South of Iran. It is the route for oil transport.

4. Strait in Other Areas

Turkey Strait is the only connection line between the Black Sea and the Mediterranean Sea. It is the separation between the European Continent and the Asian Continent. There are three parts, including Istanbul Strait (Bosporus Strait), Sea of Marmara, and Dardanelles Strait. It connects the Black Sea, Sea of Marmara, and Aegean Sea. And it connects the Mediterranean Sea via the Aegean Sea.

V. Marine Territory of China

China is a powerful country in her oceans. There are four seas, namely Bohai, Huanghai (the Yellow Sea), East China Sea, and South China Sea. We have neighbouring countries connecting via seawater, such countries like Vietnam, the Democratic People's Republic of Korea, the Republic of Korea, Japan, the Philippines, Brunei, Malaysia, and Indonesia. A variety of ships sail in those waters every day.

1. Bohai

Bohai is the inland water of China. Liaoning province, Hebei province, Shandong province, and Tianjin city surround it. The separation of Bohai and Huanghai is on the line joining between Penglai Jiao (Penglai Cape) of Shandong Province and Laotie Shan of Liaoning Province. The west part of the line is Bohai while the east part of the line is

Huanghai. Amongst the four seas in China. Bohai is the minimum.

2. Huanghai (the Yellow Sea)

Huanghai (the Yellow Sea) is a sea surrounded by the coastline of China, and the coastline of Korean Peninsula. The further north is Liaodong Bandao of China. As silt is from Huanghe (the Yellow River) or other river concentrates, the colour of the water becomes yellow and salt density is lower than other seas. In China, the sea level is calculated on the basis of the sea level of Huanghai.

3. East China Sea

The separation of Huanghai and East China Sea is a line joining between North Cape of Changjiangkou (the mouth of the Yangtze River) of China and southwest of Cheju Island of the Republic of Korea. Diaoyu Dao (钓鱼岛) which belongs to the People's Republic of China is located in East China Sea.

4. South China Sea

South China Sea was named Zhanghai (涨海) and it was the first time for human beings to name South China Sea. All the areas including lands and water within 9 dash lines are territories of China. The separation between East China Sea and South China Sea is the line joining between Nanao Dao(南澳岛) of Guangdong Province and Eluanbi (鹅銮鼻) of the southpoint of Taiwan Province. There are several *Qundaos* (群岛), many *Daos* (岛), *Yues* (屿), *Zhous* (洲), *Jiaos* (礁), *Shis* (石), *Tans* (滩) in South China Sea. For example, Huangyan Dao (黄岩岛) and Zengmuan Sha (曾母暗沙) are the lands of China. South China Sea is full of fishing resources, mining resources, natural gas resources, etc. South China Sea is also significant in merchant shipping, as several important shipping routes pass through South China Sea.

VI. Related Culture Words and Technical Terms

canal culture (运河文化)—It is the culture formed by Da Yunhe. President Xi Jinping visited a canal culture park located in Shaoxing. He stressed that the Grand Canal is the world's longest artificial waterway, and the culture related to the canal is an important part of the fine traditional Chinese culture and demands proper protection, inheritance and utilization.

caoyun (*n.*) (漕运)—Water transport of grains, salt, or other important goods by Da Yunhe. It is a type of official transport in water. In the Tang, the Song, the Yuan, the Ming, and the Qing dynasties, Caoyun was paid much attention. Caoyun was ceased in Guang Xu No.27 (1901).

Wade-Gile system (威妥玛拼音)—It is Chinese Pinyin system created by Wade-Gile in the middle of the 19th century. It was used to name places in China. Nowadays, it has been replaced by Chinese Pinyin.

VII. Exercises

1. Discuss with your classmates and answer the following questions.

1）Why is the first largest ocean called the Pacific Ocean?

2）Why is the second largest ocean called the Atlantic Ocean?

3）Why is the third largest ocean called the Indian Ocean?

4）Why is the Arctic Ocean not called the North Ice Ocean?

5）Why is Huanghai called the Yellow Sea?

6）What is the major difference between the canal and the river?

7）What is called the North Polar Route?

8）Compare the lengths of voyages between Dalian to Sanya and Dalian to Nagasaki Which is called a coastal voyage?

9）Which water is deepest in the world?

10）How many percentage of water is there in the world?

2. Deep thinking.

1）Why do we say Diaoyu Dao is the English name for "钓鱼岛" and Diaoyu Island is not the correct English name?

2）Check the separations among Europe, Africa, and Asia Continents.

3）Why do we confirm that Huangyan Dao belongs to China?

4）What organization is responsible for controlling the naming of places in China?

5）If the Suez Canal is blocked, where can the ship detour from East Asia to West Europe?

6）Design a passage from Shanghai to Amsterdam.

7）If you greet a businessman in London in 1700 Beijing Standard Time, what greeting word will you use, good morning or good afternoon? Why?

8）Describe the similarities in shapes among Taiwan Dao, Tasmania Island, and Madagascar Island.

9）Describe the importance of the Canal Culture in China.

10）Describe the English words for strait.

3. Translate the following sentences into English.

1）中国是一个幅员辽阔的国家,中国的海洋疆土也位于世界前列,我们有完全属于中国自己的内海,即渤海。此外我们还有黄海、东海、南海。

2）"峡湾地貌"是一种冰川侵蚀地貌,是冰川下滑到海平面附近而形成的山岳冰川,形成峡湾地貌的区域一定是高纬度沿海地区。

3）海峡是指两个水域之间的狭窄水上通道,它不仅是海上交通要道、航运枢纽,而且历来是兵家必争之地,人称海上交通"咽喉"。

4）珊瑚是珊瑚虫分泌出来的外壳,主要由碳酸钙组成。珊瑚礁是珊瑚骨骼在成百上千年的生长中堆积形成的。经年累月后,珊瑚群体内的骨骼累积量相当可观,加上其他生物如贝类、石灰藻、有孔虫等也会分泌钙质骨骼,胶结在一起便逐渐形成大块的礁体,即所谓的"珊瑚礁"。

5）直布罗陀海峡是非洲和欧洲的分界线。直布罗陀海峡位于西班牙最南部和非洲西北部之间,最窄处在西班牙马罗基角和摩洛哥西雷斯角之间,宽仅 14 千米。直布罗陀海峡是连接地中海和大西洋的重要门户。

4. Translate the following sentences into Chinese.

1) The Name of the Pacific Ocean was created by Navigator Ferdinand Magellan since there was a calm sea while his fleet transited it. The English Name Atlantic was borrowed from the Greek and it means the Sea of Atlas. Latin, the Atlantic Ocean is called "Mare Atlanticum". In Greek, it is called "Atlantis".

2) The travelling system of the Grand Canal was established via the Canal during the long history. It embodies ancient Chinese intelligence in making use of water system as well. In the very ancient period, Da Yu Zhi Shui(大禹治水) story shows Yu used a guidance approach in order to control the flooding. It was a great creature in combination with ancient Chinese economy, communications, culture, and civilization. In short, the Grand Canal is the heritage of the Chinese and we are proud of the Grand Canal.

3) The Arctic was originated from the Greek. Bernhardus Varenius (1622 – 1650), German named it which means the Ocean faced to the Great Bear (Polaris). In 1845, the London Geographical Committee named as the Arctic Ocean.

4) There is very little known about Biscay Bay before 1845, but most of the land area of Biscay Bay was owned by William D. Jackson, an English merchant, when Thomas Ryan of Trepassey (originally from Ireland) went to live there in that year. Other families at the time were the Easemans and Whites.

5) The Baltic Sea is an arm of the Atlantic Ocean, enclosed by Denmark, Estonia, Finland, Latvia, Lithuania, Sweden, northeast Germany, Poland, Russia and the North and Central European Plain.

Lesson 22   Introductions to Port or Harbour
第 22 课   港口介绍

In the maritime English, there are a few words shared similar meanings for ports, such as harbour, jetty, berth, wharf, pier, dock, quay, terminal, etc.

I . Meanings of the Words

A port or a seaport is a connection between the land and the sea. It is similar to the Chinese word "津". For example, the original meaning of "天津" refers to the connection among sky, water, and the land.

A harbour is a large place for sea transport service. A harbour may include the Port Authority Office, railway terminal, wharfs, berths, etc. To some extent, harbour is similar to ports.

A jetty is a wooden or stone structure which is built in the water at the edge of a sea or lake and is used by people getting on and off boats. A jetty is a berthing place which protrudes seaward. In another word, not all berths can be called jetty.

A terminal is a berthing place for large vessel mooring, such as VLCCs, ULCCs, cruise ships, etc. Unlike jetty, the terminal is much far away from the land. In other word, terminal is located at the end of the trestle.

A dock is a part of a port, etc. where ships go for loading, unloading or repair, especially one fitted with gates to control the water level area with docks and equipment for building and repairing ships. A dock is a berthing place for ship refit and repair. For example, dry dock is the place for the ship bottom repair. Dock is normally located in the shipyard.

A berth refers to a place for ship mooring. Maybe the berth is similar to mooring place for a ship.

A pier structure of wood, iron, etc. built out into the sea, a lake, etc. so that boats can stop and take on or put down passengers or goods.

A wharf is a landing place or pier where ships may tie up and load or unload. The we may imagine it as the word warehouse. The warehouse is a place in which goods or merchandise are stored. Perhaps we can say the wharf is a berth with warehouse, etc.

II . Types of Ports

In accordance with the locations, ports are classified into sea ports, river ports, lake ports, and reservoir ports. Sea ports are the largest ports amongst those.

In accordance with the functions, ports are divided into merchant ports, fishing ports, military ports, sheltered ports, dangerous goods ports, passenger ports, cargo ports, etc.

Facilities in Ports

In general, a port includes port authority office, stevedore company office, mooring station, pilot station, warehouses, railway and highway terminals, lifting facilities, passenger arrival and departure lounge, places for immigration, quarantine, and customs, etc.

III. Famous Seaports in China

There are many famous or important seaports in China, for example, Dandong, Yingkou, Dalian, and Jinzhou in Liaoning Province; Qinhuangdao, Caofeidian, and Huanghua in Hebei Province; Longkou, Yantai, Weihai, Qingdao, and Rizhao in Shandong Province; Lianyungang, Zhenjiang, Nantong in Jiangsu Province; Ningbo, Zhoushan in Zhejiang Province; Fuzhou, Xiamen, Quanzhou in Fujian Province; Guangzhou, Shenzhen, Zhanjiang, Shantou, Zhuhai in Guangdong Province; Fangcheng, Beihai, and Qinzhou in Guangxi Zhuang Autonomous Region, Jilong, Hualian, and Gaoxiong in Taiwan Province; Haikou, Sanya, and Basuo in Hainan Province, etc.

IV. Famous Seaports Overseas

There are important Seaports located in Asia. Examples are Tokyo (Japan), Yokohama (Japan), Kobe (Japan), Osaka (Japan), Chiba (Japan), Huchiming City (Vietnam), Singapore (Singapore), Manila (the Philippines), Jakarta (Indonesia), Colombo (Malaysia), Busan (ROK), Mokpo (ROK), Kwangyang (ROK), Ulsan (ROK), Yosu (ROK), Bangkok (Thailand), Mumbai or Bombay (India), Kolkata (India), Rangoon (Myanmar), Moulmein (Myanmar), Dubai (United Arab Emirates), Dammam (Saudi Arabia), Riyadh (Saudi Arabia), Kuwait (Kuwait), etc.

There are also important seaports located in Europe. For instance, Amsterdam (Netherland), Rotterdam (Netherland), Antwerp (Belgium), Hamburg (Germany), Oslo (Norway), Bergen (Norway), Stockholm (Sweden), Copenhagen (Denmark), etc.

The famous ports in Australia and New Zealand include Sydney (Australia), Canberra (Australia), Melbourne (Australia), Auckland (New Zealand), Napier (New Zealand), Tauranga (New Zealand), Wellington (New Zealand), etc.

In Africa, the famous sea ports are Durban (South Africa), Capetown (South Africa), Port Elizabeth (South Africa), Mombasa (Mozambique), Port Said (Egypt), Alexandria (Egypt), Dakar (Senegal), Nouakchott (Mauretania), Tunis (Tunis), Algiers (Algeria), etc.

In America, the famous and important ports are Vancouver (Canada), Halifax (Canada), New York (USA), Los Angles (USA), Seattle (USA), Oakland, (USA) Savannah (USA), Valparaiso (Chile), Tumaco (Colombia), Rio De Janeiro (Brazil), Santos (Brazil), Callao (Peru), Buenos Airs (Argentina), Montevideo (Uruguay), Panama City (Panama), San Jose (Guatemala), etc.

V. Related Culture Words and Technical Terms

Pidgin English (洋泾浜英语)—It is a dialect of English formed from 16th century. Ports are places to form those special dialects of English. It was said that the word pidgin was from Chinese word Peiqian(赔钱). Therefore, pidgin English is a kind of business English. Nowadays, pidgin English almost disappeared because of the education.

longshoreman (*n.*) (码头工, 装卸工)—Workers for cargo loading or discharging in ports. It is a type of American English.

stevedore (*n.*) (码头工, 装卸工)—Workers for cargo loading or discharging in ports. It is a type of British English.

bay (*n.*)(港湾)—A metaphor to describe one of the functions of ports. It offers the peaceful and safe places for ships in order to prevent wind and currents, or other heavy weather.

harbour basin (港池)—A water place enclosed by the coast line and the breakwater.

entrance of breakwater (防波堤口门)—A place where the inbound and outbound vessels transit.

farewell buoy (告别浮筒)—The furthest buoy from the coast. For the outbound vessel, it is the farewell buoy. For inbound vessel, it is the welcome buoy.

roadstead(*n.*) (港外锚地)—It is the horn shaped anchorage outside of the port. This term was borrowed from COLREG 72.

anchorage (*n.*) (锚地)—A place located the outside of a port. It may be divided into standby anchorage, sheltered anchorage, quarantine anchorage, and dangerous goods anchorage according to the functions.

VI. Exercises

1. Discuss with your classmates and answer the following questions.

1) List five important ports in Japan.

2) List important ports in Russia.

3) List five important ports in the Republic of Korea.

4) List different types of ports.

5) List important ports in Australia and New Zealand.

6) List important ports in European Countries.

7) List five large sea ports in China.

8) List important ports in South America.

9) List important ports in Africa.

10) List important ports in North America.

2. Deep thinking.

1) What does "津" stand for?

2) What does the word port mean? Explain the meanings of port in seaport and airport.

3) Why do we use terminal in oil terminal?

4) What does the word jetty stand for? Where does the term jetty apply for?

5）What does dry dock mean? Why do we use the term in the shipping repair?

6）Please look up information on China Ports and Harbours Association.

7）How is the Chinese "舫" translated into English?

8）List important relay ports in the Pacific Ocean. Explain the importance of those ports.

9）Look up a dictionary and compare words—berth, wharf, jetty, pier, dock, quay, terminal, and pontoon.

10）List common port facilities.

3. Translate the following sentences into English.

1）港口设施包括防波堤、港口装卸货设施、港口仓储、泊位、港口建筑、铁路等。

2）港口通常开埠在江河湖海沿岸，是重要的交通枢纽，围绕港口还开发了其他服务。

3）最原始的港口是天然港口，有天然掩护的海湾、水湾、河口等场所供船舶停泊。

4）现代化的港口有各种形态，可以从不同角度定义港口，比如按照用途，港口可以分为商港、军港、渔港、避风港等。

5）有关港口词汇可以从全国科技名词审定委员会的"术语在线"的网站上查询，其网站是 www.termonline.cn/。

4. Translate the following sentences into Chinese.

1）A port is a maritime facility which may comprise one or more wharves where ships may dock to load and discharge passengers and cargo. Although usually situated on a sea coast or estuary, some ports, such as Hamburg, Manchester and Duluth, are many miles inland, with access to the sea via river or canal.

2）Because of the roles of ports as a port of entry for immigrants many port cities such as London, New York, Los Angeles, Singapore and Vancouver have experienced dramatic multi-ethnic and multicultural changes.

3）In ancient Greece, Athens' port of Piraeus was the base for the Athenian fleet which played a crucial role in the Battle of Salamis against the Persians in 480 BCE.

4）A harbor（American English）or a harbour（British English; see spelling differences）（synonym: haven）is a sheltered body of water where ships, boats, and barges can be docked. The term harbour is often used interchangeably with port, which is a man-made facility built for loading and unloading vessels and dropping off and picking up passengers.

5）A natural harbour is a landform where a section of a body of water is protected and deep enough to allow anchorage. Natural harbours have long been of great strategic naval and economic importance, and many great cities of the world are located on them. Having a protected harbour reduces or eliminates the need for breakwaters as it will result in calmer waves inside the harbour.

参考文献

1. 图书

[1] PIKE D. The history of navigation[M]. UK：Pen & Sword Maritime，2018.

[2] GILES O C，G N JJ，DEBATTISTA C，etc. Shipping law[M]. 8th ed. UK：Pitman Publishing，1987.

[3] 何庆华,吕红光. 航海概论[M]. 大连:大连海事大学出版社,2014.

[4] 李伟. 船舶结构与设备[M]. 大连:大连海事大学出版社,2013.

[5] 张晓峰. 航运管理实务及翻译实践[M]. 大连:大连海事大学出版社,2022.

[6] 张晓峰,张君彦,王浩亮,等. 修船实用英语[M]. 大连:大连海事大学出版社,2017.

[7] 张晓峰. 造船实用英语[M]. 大连:大连海事大学出版社,2017.

2. 网络

[1] 人民日报.习近平在浙江考察时强调 始终干在实处走在前列勇立潮头 奋力谱写中国式现代化浙江新篇章（2023-09-26）［2024-03-18］.http://paper.people.com.cn/rmrb/html/2023-09/26/nw.D110000renmrb_20230926_2-01.htm

[2] China Daily. Nation's modernization drive attracts global attention.（2023-05-10）［2024-03-18］.https://www.chinadaily.com.cn/a/202305/10/WS645ad2dea310b6054fad2018.html

[3] China Daily. Strategy benefits all with 'endless potential'.（2023-04-28）［2024-03-18］. https://epaper.chinadaily.com.cn/a/202304/28/WS644b0016a310b1dea957e221.html